The Fragrance of Knowledge

by
Janet Lay

The Fragrance of Knowledge, Second Edition
Copyright © of Second Edition, 2001
Copyright © of First Edition, 1982
ISBN 0-88144-221-6
Janet Lay
Faith Family Ministries
3119 Buffalo Lane
Grove, Oklahoma 74344 U.S.A.

Published by:
Christian Publishing Services
P. O. Box 701434
Tulsa, OK 74170

Text design: Lisa Simpson

Endorsements

Fragrance of Knowledge is a tool of the Lord to equip women to be all they are called to be in their own lives in the roles God has given them in their family.

Janet Lay is a gifted, anointed, and compassionate woman of God. I have personally ministered with Janet for several years on many occasions and have seen the obvious change in the lives of those she touched through her teaching. Many women today are living victorious lives because of her faithfulness to believe and stand upon the Word of God for their lives. Many families are strong today because of the teaching contained in this book.

Janet's life reflects the "knowledge" she has written in this book. She is truly an example of a godly woman. She is a faithful and wonderful friend.

Pam Mickler, Co-pastor
Victory Christian Center
Lafayette, Indiana

Janet Lay has been a true mentor to me. Not only has her *Fragrance of Knowledge* enhanced our marriage, her encouragement helped me step out and begin a Bible study that has blessed hundreds of ladies.

Janet is one of our favorite speakers. When she comes to minister to us, she always has a fresh word from the Lord.

Dorothy Enns
Dorothy & Friends Bible Study
Tulsa, Oklahoma

I have heard Janet Lay teach *Fragrance of Knowledge* several times in the past. She has not deviated from the original mandate that God gave her – to help bring families back to the God-given plan for the family on earth which is to represent the heavenly family.

Janet's whole life is based on "worship God and love people." It is my opinion that she knows the heart of God as He expressed in First Peter 3:7:

> In the same way you married men should live considerately with [your wives], with an intelligent recognition [of the marriage relation], honoring the woman as [physically] the weaker, but [realizing that you] are joint heirs of the grace (God's unmerited favor) of life, in order that your prayers may not be hindered and cut off. [Otherwise you cannot pray effectively.]

Alnita Cypert
Grove, Oklahoma

Dedication

I dedicate this book to Bill Lay,
my loving husband of fifty years,
who has stood by my side loving me
and patiently teaching me so many things
as I learned how to be
a godly helpmeet to him.

Also, to the memory of my parents,
Harvey and Katherine Sparkman,
who taught me Christian values
that helped me to be a godly woman.

Acknowledgment

I wish to thank Georgia Jackson,
my mother-in-love,
who taught me by example
the art of good homemaking.
I love you, Mom!

I thank Alnita Cypert,
my friend and sister in the Lord,
who transcribed my teaching tapes
and helped me in the preparation
of this book.
Thank you, Alnita.

Rev. Bill & Janet Lay

Foreword

by Sharon Daugherty
Co-pastor, Victory Christian Center
Tulsa, Oklahoma

My husband and I have known Bill and Janet Lay for twenty-six years. Janet has taught solid biblical truths on marriage and the family throughout the years I have known her. Her own testimony has shown how a Christian can apply Scripture to his or her marriage relationship and see it glorify God and help others.

Janet gives personal insight into relating the Word of God to society today. God's Word is still relevant. Isaiah 33:6 KJV says that **"wisdom and knowledge shall be the stability of thy times, and strength of salvation: the fear of the Lord is his treasure."** Janet relates God's Word as His wisdom and knowledge to stabilize our lives. Marriages and families are being shaken today where God's wisdom and knowledge are not being sought.

Our strength will rise or fall according to whether or not we recognize our need for His truth in our lives daily and whether or not we walk in the fear of the Lord. I encourage you to open your heart and let God speak to you as you read this book. For those who have good marriages and family relationships, it will affirm and strengthen you. For those who may be in need of healing, it will bring healing and help to you.

I believe as you read, you'll be inspired, healed, instructed, lovingly corrected, and encouraged to release your faith in God's Word and obey Him.

Preface

In 1982, after I had been teaching on marriage and family for some years, the Holy Spirit began to minister to me that He wanted me to write a course – the course that I had been teaching, and include my own experiences.

I began to pray about it, and as I did, I had a telephone call from a lady who, with her sister, had attended my class at Sheridan Christian Center, Tulsa, Oklahoma. Both had been born again. The next course I taught was at the Methodist Church, and they brought their mother, who was born again and had been delivered from an alcoholic condition. This family was really turned on to God.

One day Bobette, the daughter, called and said, "Janet, there is a strange thing happening to my mother." When I asked what was happening, she said, "Well, we were walking in the River Parks the other day and Mother said, "Bobette, you see the people walking there? They are Christians." I said, "Now, Mother, how can you tell they are Christians?"

The mother said, "Don't you smell that sweet aroma?" Bobette answered, "No."

A few days later they were in a grocery store and the mother said, "Bobette, those two people are Christians and that one (pointing) is a better Christian than the other."

She said, "Now, Mother, don't tell me that you are smelling Christians again."

The mother said, "Yes, can't you smell that sweet aroma?"

I didn't have any answer for Bobette as I had never heard of it before in my life. But a few days later I got a magazine from a ministry in my mailbox. It had a rose and Second Corinthians 2:14 on the cover. This is where I took the title, *The Fragrance of Knowledge,* for my course.

This is the commission that God placed upon my life at that time, and even though I was the pastor's wife and loved it, I wouldn't do anything else. We know that God put us at Cornerstone Church, Grove, Oklahoma, for a season, but my first love is that of ministering to women. God has never released me from that commission.

When I teach in women's conferences or retreats, it is like there is a strong anointing upon my life to cause women to stand up and begin to walk in the freedom of Christ Jesus. God said, "I want you to go and minister My love and My knowledge to women so that every place they go, whether they are in their workplace or at home, women can become that sweet-smelling fragrance."

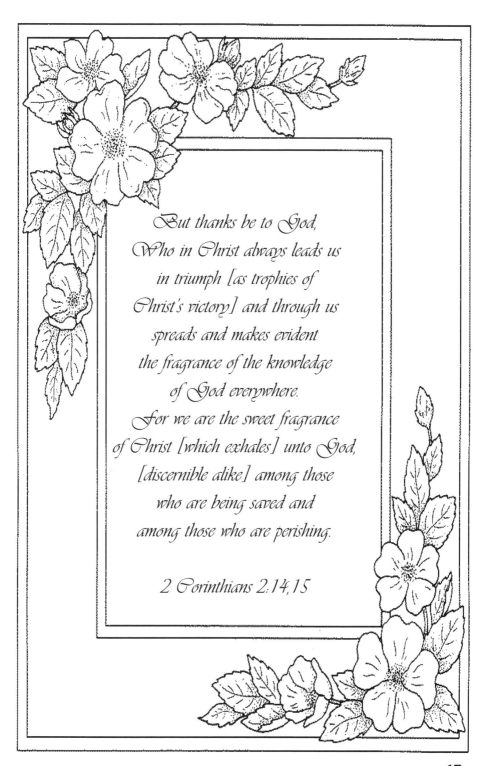

But thanks be to God,
Who in Christ always leads us
in triumph [as trophies of
Christ's victory] and through us
spreads and makes evident
the fragrance of the knowledge
of God everywhere.
For we are the sweet fragrance
of Christ [which exhales] unto God,
[discernible alike] among those
who are being saved and
among those who are perishing.

2 Corinthians 2:14,15

Introduction

When Bill and I married, he thought that I was the very best thing that had happened in his life because he was from a family that had been broken. After we had been married twenty years, he no longer felt this way and no longer wanted to be married to me. Even though we were going to church, working in the church, and raising four sons, we found ourselves going in separate directions.

Hosea 4:6 says, **"My people are destroyed for lack of knowledge,"** and we were perishing.

I was raised in a Christian home with a large family. Bill was a Christian, but he was from a very small family. The root problem in all relationships is selfishness. We were complete opposites, with no marriage counseling, and our marriage was in trouble, even though we had assumed that we would live happily ever after.

After twenty years of marriage, we were bankrupt in every area of our lives. Our marriage was gone, our finances were gone, my husband's health was broken, and our sons were in rebellion. Nothing in our lives was good. The only good was that both of us had given our hearts to Jesus. We really wanted to serve Him, *but we were perishing for lack of knowledge.*

We were now separated. There was no one else involved in our relationship. We said we were just too different. Our relationship was not the way we knew God intended a marriage relationship to be.

Our pastor called, saying, "I have been missing you at church. Why haven't you been there?" I started to give him all the excuses that pastors are used to hearing: "The kids have been sick." "We have been out of town." But out of my mouth came, "Bill and I are separated." He was very surprised.

You see, we had our church face, we had our business face, we had our social face, and we had our face at home. All these faces looked good, except the one at home.

When the pastor asked, "Would you come to see me?" I said, "Well, I don't know. I will ask Bill." When Bill left, he had told me, "I don't love you anymore. I will support you and the boys, but I am not going to live with you."

It had come to the point where he just didn't have any hope of things being better. I was very controlling. I was very nagging. I controlled everything in the home, not knowing that was wrong. I had a very wonderful Christian mother, but she was a strong leader and she was in charge.

We went to our pastor for counseling. We had resigned our positions at the church at that time. Bill had been the Sunday school superintendent, and I was the children's church leader.

When we got into the counseling session, I said, very self-righteously, "Bill has all the complaints. Let him tell you what is wrong."

Well, for what appeared to be an eternity, my husband dumped everything right on the pastor's desk. He was very broken because he was very hurt. I thought the things he told the pastor were a bunch of non-truths. Later, I found out that it was the attitude, the way you say things, and the way you talk about things, that affects how the other person hears them.

When it was my time to share, the only thing I could share about was my mother-in-law, because I had to have some kind of defense mechanism. So I shared that Bill was an only child and I felt his relationship with his mother was too close. I found out later that my mother-in-law was not my problem – it was my attitude. She is wonderful, and she became my mother-in-love. I would not have my husband if it were not for her. She is the one who gave me that gift, so I appreciate her and love her. We have a wonderful relationship today.

So the pastor, though he was a precious man of God, had a lack of knowledge on how to counsel us. Actually, he did not give us any counsel. He did not even open the Bible to Ephesians 5. He didn't tell us anything that was in the Word of God.

I invited my husband to come home for lunch that day. It was in the month of February, and he came home. Not knowing that I was being led by the Holy Spirit, because at that stage I was forty years old, I knew about three scriptures – Jesus wept, John 3:16, and maybe one more. I did not know the Word of God like I know it today.

I had been to Bible college. I had read the Bible through many times. I had been filled with the Holy Spirit. (I knew Acts 2:4 that tells about the Holy Spirit and speaking in tongues), but I did not apply the Word of God to my life like I do now. I read it like a history book instead of a how-to book. I didn't apply the principles of the Word of God in my life because if they taught me, I did not hear them. A lot of times that is the case. I am not blaming anyone else, because I had the Holy Spirit and the Word of God right there and I could have learned.

During lunch I said to him, "Bill, what is there about me that you can't live with?" And he gave me a list! I remember saying to him, "I don't know if I can do all these things, but I love you. I really would like for you to come home."

He did come home. I would like to tell you that we lived happily ever after, but we didn't because we had the same lack of knowledge. But it was line upon line, precept upon precept (Isaiah 28:10) that we began to learn and open our hearts to the Word of God.

The pastor had said, "The root problem in all relationships is selfishness, people wanting their own way. If people would be obedient to what the Word of God says about relationships, there would not be broken relationships. Both of you have too many blessings," because both of us had talked about our families.

What we learned, I want to share with you in this book.

Janet Lay

Chapter 1

In 1986, we found our lives bankrupt in every area – health, finances, family, and spiritually. We needed help. There were not many books on Christian marriage. I think Larry Christensen's, *The Christian Family,* was on the bookshelves and maybe Pat and Shirley Boone's book on the Christian family. Also, there were not a lot of pastors or churches teaching on marriage. We did not find any marriage counsel.

Hosea 4:6 says God's people are destroyed for lack of knowledge, and we were perishing. If you read Hosea, it is a story about Gomer and Hosea,[1] and has to do with a very stormy relationship. I believe relationships perish for lack of knowledge. The book of Hosea ends with God's promise of healing and restoration.

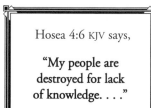

Hosea 4:6 KJV says,

"My people are destroyed for lack of knowledge. . . ."

Two people totally opposite meet and they decide to get married. If they have not had any premarital counseling or if they do not have an understanding, they go into the relationship thinking they will live happily ever after. But "after every wedding comes a marriage that has to be worked on." I believe some of the principles that the

---

[1] "Hosea" means the Lord saves or delivers.

Holy Spirit taught us were because there was not that much counseling available. But the Holy Spirit began to take us line upon line to teach us the principles of abundant living.

We changed churches for a reason that I will discuss later. This church had a wonderful Christian lady teaching the young married couples, but my husband did not believe in women teachers. So we ended up not going to church for several years, but then we went back to Sheridan Christian Center. The lady was still the teacher. We sat in that class and it was different. That is the church where Rhema Bible Training Center started and where Kenneth E. Hagin held the first indoor campmeeting. The faith movement, the charismatic movement, started and we got to be a part of that beginning.

From then on, we began to learn the things and ways of God, and we began to study to show ourselves approved. The first book I read was by Anita Bryant, *Bless This House*. Although Anita divorced, there were a lot of good principles in her book. In addition to reading Pat and Shirley Boone's book on the family and Larry Christensen's, *The Christian Family*, I read Kenneth E. Hagin's book, *Authority of the Believer*. I really began to absorb the truths of the Word of God.

> Marriages may be made in heaven, but the maintenance is up to the couple.

Our lives began to change, but it wasn't enough just to read the books. We had to be doers of the Word of God. Even though we had been separated, my husband came back home. We still had problems. Bill didn't change too much to start with because I was still controlling. I was still dominating, but little by little I began to change, and he saw the change in me. Then he began to change little things also, and here we are several years later put together by the precious blood of Jesus – the superglue of God's love – doing what we are doing today.

Bill and I loved pastoring. God put us at Cornerstone church to help people and to love them. We are a couple who has been restored, healed, set free, and launched forward to set the captives free.

Back to my story. At that time, I changed jobs and began to work with Alnita Cypert. We were invited to attend a series of classes for women only. Alnita and I started attending these classes. She did not have to cry through every class, but I did. I had done everything in the book wrong. Everything listed there I had done wrong. I have to tell you, it was ignorance on my part. I didn't know the things I was doing were wrong. So we went through the classes.

> God does not love Janet and Bill any more than He loves any person reading this book.

Out of that experience, I quit my job and traveled a couple of years with the teacher of the class, Ruth Baker. I traveled with her once a week, on Thursdays, and I listened to her. I took care of her tapes and books, and I just helped her. Occasionally she let me share a little bit and then the day came when I was asked to do a meeting as she was going to the Philippines. Next, I taught the class at the church where we attended. Then I began to teach at Victory Bible Institute, Tulsa, Oklahoma.

When I was asked to do a Women's Aglow retreat, I had never done a retreat in my life. All I could share was my testimony and the little bit which I had learned. When I went to the retreat being held at Fin and Feather Lodge, I was surprised that there were three hundred to four hundred women there. The room was packed.

I shared my testimony, and when I called for ladies to come forth, out of the three hundred to four hundred ladies, I would say that 85 to 90 percent of them came forward for ministry. I thought, *What am I going to do with this?* I mean, I backed up and the Spirit of the Lord spoke to me and said, "The same Spirit that is in Brother Hagin, Oral Roberts, or any other minister is in you." I said, "Okay," and stepped down off the platform. I began to lay hands on people and pray for them. They began to fall out and we had a mighty move of God.

As we were walking back to our cabin that night, the lady who invited me, Charlene Kinard, from Bartlesville, Oklahoma, said, "When did you start ministering like this?" And I said, "Tonight!"

So God has moved us line upon line, precept upon precept. If you are faithful over the little things, He will make you ruler over the greater. Many times people want to start at the top and not be faithful over the little things God has given them to do. Out of that retreat, we began to minister and do retreats. I realized that God has an answer for every situation and circumstance.

Controlling Spirit – Strong Will

I mentioned earlier that because of my background, I was controlling. If you look in Genesis, when Satan tempted Eve, he didn't tempt her because she was hungry. There were things all over the garden to eat. He told her that if she would eat of this one tree, **"You will be like God, knowing the difference between good and evil and blessing and calamity"** (Genesis 3:5). It had to do with position.

I believe that from the beginning of time women have had to deal with control and manipulation. A lot of times when I have taught this course, women will say, "It looks like manipulation." Because when you begin to admire your husband and treat him in that manner, then good things begin to happen to you. I often say to women, "You don't have to be taught how to manipulate. You knew how to manipulate from the time you found out that you were a little girl." Look how little girls manipulate their daddies. Most daddies do anything a little girl wants.

> We don't have to be taught manipulation. We have to be taught that our heart motives should be right and to do our husbands only good as long as there is life within us.

One time before we moved to Grove, we were at home. Our oldest granddaughter, Amy, was about three. She called on the phone one day and said, "Grandma, can I talk to Poppy?" I said, "Honey, Poppy is working in the garage this evening. Would you like to talk to Grandma?"

I started asking her questions. She was very polite and answered my questions, but she said, "Grandma, can I talk to Poppy now?"

I went to the garage door and said, "Poppy, your number one granddaughter (we only had one at the time) wants to talk to you." He came to the phone and all she said was, "Poppy, I don't have any pink jellies," which were little plastic shoes. He said, "Well, Honey, where do we get pink jellies?" "They are at C. R. Anthony's." He said, "Okay, Poppy will be over there in about an hour, and we will get you some jellies."

Everything was laid aside. Poppy and Grandma went to Anthony's store, found the jellies, and took them to Amy. *Little girls know how to manipulate.*

Even quiet women will be controllers because they control by being quiet, as Eve did in the garden. I believe that from the beginning of time, women have had to deal with control and manipulation.

Gossiping Spirit

Back to my story. As I said before, we started going to another church, not because of the pastor. It was just that by the time we went into his office and shared regarding our situation, very quickly the fact that we had a problem and were separated began to spread among the church members. If you want to know why I am so hard on gossip, this is one of the reasons.

Even if you are telling the truth, it can be a destroying factor in a person's life. I am saying to you that death and life are in the tongue,[2] and you need not be a weapon formed against somebody else because you are carrying tales even if they are true.

I remember a situation several years ago where I watched this woman who would go from person to person sharing a situation. So on a Sunday evening, I watched her go to another lady in the church

---

[2] Proverbs 11:13 KJV - "A talebearer revealeth secrets, but he that is of a faithful spirit concealeth the matter." Proverbs 18:8 KJV - "The words of a talebearer are as wounds, and they go down into the innermost parts of the belly." Proverbs 26:20 KJV - "Where no wood is, there the fire goeth out: so where there is no talebearer, the strife ceaseth."

and take her to the restroom. I knew she was getting ready to give her this tale. I gave them time to get started on the gossip, then I went into the restroom. I said to the lady, and I say it to you, knowing what gossip can do, "Cornerstone is a church of love, acceptance, and forgiveness, but you cannot come to this church and gossip. That is one of the things we will not allow."

If you are gossiping, you are sinning and you need to ask God to forgive you. I don't care if you know something negative about someone, you need to take it to the Lord in prayer. If you find out something, you have no business sharing it with anyone else because you become the weapon formed against that situation, and the Word of God says you will not prosper. Gossip is deadly.

Anyway, our marital situation was talked about, and we didn't feel comfortable going back to our former church. We loved the pastor and we loved the people as we had served there, but we changed churches.

I believe with godly people, their steps are ordered by the Lord. We started attending Sheridan Christian Center, Tulsa, Oklahoma.

Personal Character and Value

A capable, intelligent, and virtuous woman – who is he who can find her? She is far more precious than jewels and her value is far above rubies or pearls.

The heart of her husband trusts in her confidently and relies on and believes in her securely, so that he has no lack of [honest] gain or need of [dishonest] spoil.

She comforts, encourages, and does him only good as long as there is life within her.

She seeks out wool and flax and works with willing hands [to develop it].

She is like the merchant ships loaded with foodstuffs; she brings her household's food from a far [country].

She rises while it is yet night and gets [spiritual] food for her household and assigns her maids their tasks.

She considers a [new] field before she buys or accepts it [expanding prudently and not courting neglect of her present duties by assuming other duties]; with her savings [of time and strength] she plants fruitful vines in her vineyard.

She girds herself with strength [spiritual, mental, and physical fitness for her God-given task] and makes her arms strong and firm.

She tastes and sees that her gain from work [with and for God] is good; her lamp goes not out, but it burns on continually through the night [of trouble, privation, or sorrow, warning away fear, doubt, and distrust].

She lays her hands to the spindle, and her hands hold the distaff.

She opens her hand to the poor, yes, she reaches out her filled hands to the needy [whether in body, mind, or spirit].

She fears not the snow for her family, for all her household are doubly clothed in scarlet.

She makes for herself coverlets, cushions, and rugs of tapestry. Her clothing is of linen, pure and fine, and of purple [such as that of which the clothing of the priests and the hallowed cloths of the temple were made].

Her husband is known in the [city's] gates, when he sits among the elders of the land.

She makes fine linen garments and leads others to buy them; she delivers to the merchants girdles for sashes that free one up for service].

Strength and dignity are her clothing and her position is strong and secure; she rejoices over the future [the latter day or time to come, knowing that she and her family are in readiness for it]!

She opens her mouth in skillful and godly Wisdom, and on her tongue is the law of kindness [giving counsel and instruction].

She looks well to how things go in her household, and the bread of idleness (gossip, discontent, and self-pity) she will not eat.

Her children rise up and call her blessed (happy, fortunate, and to be envied); and her husband boasts of and praises her, [saying],

Many daughters have done virtuously, nobly, and well [with the strength of character that is steadfast in goodness], but you excel them all.

Charm and grace are deceptive, and beauty is vain [because it is not lasting], but a woman who reverently and worshipfully fears the Lord, she shall be praised!

Give her of the fruit of her hands, and let her own works praise her in the gates [of the city]!

Proverbs 31:10-31

I want you to take note of verse 10: **"A capable, intelligent, and virtuous woman – who is he who can find her? . . ."** I realize that when we read these scripture verses, it seems like it is not humanly possible to fulfill these goals. I believe that every characteristic that is described in these verses lies within us. I do not believe God is any respecter of persons. I believe you have everything you need to be a success in life. You have these characteristics in you. You might say, "Well, this is the perfect woman." No, it isn't!

Some writers feel, and I agree with them, that Solomon wrote this about Bathsheba, his mother. Bathsheba made some big mistakes in her life. She committed adultery with David. Now, we know that David was the king at that time. I have studied about this, and I am not so sure that she resisted his advances. The Bible says she bathed on the roof and made herself ready. Don't you think if there was a two-story house next to you and you knew someone could see you on your deck or balcony that you wouldn't be out there bathing? You would not be getting yourself ready where someone could see you.

It sounds to me like it was two-sided. I am not putting her down, but I have thought about this chemistry. We know she got pregnant. Sometimes pregnancy happens on the first time of intimacy. A lot of times it doesn't. And I am not so sure that this was a one-time situation with her and David because we know the time of the month a woman can get pregnant happens the time she desires relationship with her husband, or it should be with her husband. Her chemistry and hormones are such that she desires to have a relationship.

Bathsheba's husband was gone and she was out on the roof having a bath with David living next door. You can believe what you want, but I counsel enough to know some of these things. I don't think she did everything right, and she ended up having a child out of wedlock. Her husband was murdered to cover up the sin.

David and Bathsheba lost that child. She knew what it was to suffer the grief of losing a child. A sacrificial lamb was slain, looking forward to the sacrifice of Jesus Christ, and she found the mercy and grace of God in her life. She and David did get married, and God gave them Solomon who was the wisest man on earth before Jesus. So we know that there was restoration in her life.

I want to say to you that being a capable, intelligent, and virtuous woman does not mean that you have done everything right.

I always thought being a virtuous woman was a woman who was a virgin when she married. She has done everything right. She doesn't nag her husband. She has always told the truth. She has never had any vanity or anything like that. But I am saying to you that this is not the case. It is only through the grace of Jesus Christ that we become virtuous women.

I believe that Proverbs 31:10-31 is a very important portion of Scripture because everything that is in it is in you. As we press on toward that mark which is before us, the strength of God and the guidance of the Holy Spirit will help us become everything God wants us to be.

What Is a Virtuous Woman?

I did a study on a virtuous woman and found there was only one woman in the Bible who was called virtuous. That was Ruth.

In Ruth 3:11 she was called a virtuous woman. Ruth's husband died and we know that she chose to go with her mother-in-law. Her mother-in-law, Naomi, helped her find a new husband, Boaz. We know that Ruth was called a virtuous woman. I believe she had a good attitude. She did not allow her circumstances of losing her husband to keep her down. She chose to get up and press on to the mark which was before her and found restoration in her life.

As I studied, I asked the Lord, "What is a virtuous woman? Tell me about it." I found in the Hebrew that it means she is a woman who chooses to do right.

If you have chosen Jesus Christ as your Lord and Savior, you are doing what you can to live by His Word, and you have the precious blood of Jesus in your life. Even if you are not doing everything right, you are a virtuous woman because of what Jesus did. Every woman reading this book is a virtuous woman if she has chosen Jesus as her personal Lord and Savior because when He came into your life, He cleansed you of all your sins and mistakes. But not only that, He made a way so that if you make a mistake, it will be forgiven because of His grace. Everyone who believes has been cleansed by the precious blood of Jesus. My Bible tells me that what God has cleansed, let no one call unclean. So I call you cleansed. I say you are virtuous because you have chosen Jesus as your personal Savior.

I am a virtuous woman. More than that, I am a virtuous woman because of what Jesus did. It has nothing to do with what I did. I just had to accept what He did and that makes me a virtuous woman.

Now, let me ask you a couple of questions. Number one, Are you a virtuous woman? What are you worth as a person? I am not talking about what the chemicals in your physical body are worth, but what are you worth as a person? Question two, Are you happy and excited about who you are? Would you rather be someone else? It is important that you are honest in these things because you need to know that God made you just as you are. You see, how you answer these questions plays a key role in how you will live your life, in the joy you will experience, in the way you treat others, and in how you respond to God.

Question one – It is not so much who you are as who you think you are that determines these life responses. Proverbs 23:7 KJV says, "**For as he** [means a man or a woman] **thinketh in his** [her] **heart,**

33

so is he [she]. . . ." In Mark 12:28 KJV a scribe came and asked Jesus, **"Which is the first commandment of all?"** Jesus said, **"Thou shalt love the Lord thy God with all thy heart, and with all thy soul, and with all thy mind, and with all thy strength . . . and the second is . . . thou shalt love thy neighbour as thyself . . ."** (Mark 12:30,31 KJV). Three loves: relationship with God, relationship with yourself, then relationship with others.

You can have a relationship with God. I did for many years. I was born again when I was nine years of age, but I sat on my front porch many a time when my husband worked nights, crying, "God, why did You make me like I am? Why didn't You make me like Alnita? Why didn't You make me like Kim, or Sally, or Joan?" I didn't like myself, but I didn't know that there was anything I could do about it. I felt that everyone else was better, prettier, a better mother, or a better wife than I was.

It is very important how you feel about yourself because you judge other people exactly as you judge yourself. If you don't feel good about yourself, then you will always be going around being judgmental of other people. When you find a person who is harsh, critical, and always reaching out to slash other people, that really turns you off, doesn't it? But you need to have compassion because that person is hurting on the inside about the way they feel and see themselves.

> You cannot love other people properly unless you love yourself and see yourself as being valuable and precious.

The gauge with which you measure your love for someone else is how much you love yourself. You cannot love other people more than you love yourself. That is one of the reasons you have broken relationships. You cannot get along because of this problem.

So, the first relationship is with God and the second is with yourself, which is very important, and the third is the relationship with others.

Each person has three basic emotional needs: to love, to be loved, and to be made to feel worthwhile. I do not care whether you are a man, woman, boy, girl, old, young, or middle aged. Every person has these three basic emotional needs. This will help you to understand people.

Proverbs 24:3,4 says that through skillful and godly wisdom is a life, a family, a home built. Through understanding it is established on a sound and good foundation. So we need that knowledge, that understanding, and that wisdom to build our homes and families. Knowing the way we look at ourselves is so important, because it helps us to have good relationships with other people.

If I could see on the inside of you, open you up like a wallet or a billfold, what would I see? If your heart or your mind were opened up and someone accidentally saw on the inside, what do you think you would look like and what would they see?

Proverbs 31:10 says, **"A capable, intelligent, and virtuous woman – who is he who can find her? She is far more precious than jewels and her value is far above rubies or pearls."** The price you pay for something is what it is worth. The price that was paid for you was the precious blood of Jesus, and I do not believe God made that kind of investment in a "nobody." What He paid, money can't buy. What you have, money can't buy. It says that you are priceless. You need to know that you are priceless and that you are unique.

There are no two ladies alike. Not many women, unless you made it, have ever had an original dress, but you are originals. That makes you valuable; that makes you precious. There is no one like you. God made you with two eyes that could see and two ears that could hear. I can talk to you and my voice would be hitting the smallest bone in your body and you can hear me. That is a miracle! What has been invested in you is worth more than money can buy.

Do you have children? Let me ask you something. If someone came to your door and started telling you that your children were brats, they were no good, they would never amount to anything, or they do not have enough sense to come in out of the rain, what would you do? You would be ready to pull hair, wouldn't you?

A lot of people have been talking about God's children that way. You have been talking about yourself and you belong to God. God does not like what you have been saying about His children. He wants you to clean your mouth up and begin talking good about His children. It is very important. It is important because you can never be as effective for the Kingdom of God if you don't know how valuable you are. You are a success looking for a place to happen. You are somebody who has the anointing of God in you that the people of the world need to see.

I notice how people want to talk to a person who feels good about herself. They want to talk to you even though they may not know you. Do you know what they are trying to do? They are trying to get to Jesus who is inside of you. The Bible says if you lift Jesus up, He will draw all men unto Him. The more of God that you get on the inside of you, the more people are going to be drawn to you. When you go to Wal-Mart or are on a plane, people will want to talk to you. What they are seeing in you is Jesus.

A visiting woman came to our church, hugged me, and said, "I just love you." This was the first time she had been to our church. It was the love of God that she saw in me that she loved. It is the same with you. As you recognize that Jesus is in you and that you are a virtuous woman, it will cause people to love you. Some have not let Jesus come out yet. You still have negative attitudes and those things are not pleasing to Him. Begin to act and think about what Jesus says about you, and this will cause you to be pleasing to others. You need to get the picture on the inside of you of how Jesus sees you.

Question two – To have a good self-image and to love ourselves, is it selfish, conceit, and pride? No. To know that we have been created in the image of God, is it self-righteousness? No. We know that we are created in the very image of God because Genesis 1:26 KJV says God the Father, the Son, and the Holy Spirit said, **"Let us make man in our image. . . ."**

What do you see when you look in the mirror? Your image. Well, God said we are created in His image. I do not know how He is going to do it, but we all look like Him. I can only figure out that we have some of His characteristics in our life. Men and women, after having been married for several years, begin to look alike. The more you live together and spend time with each other, the more you are like them. The more you spend time in prayer and reading God's Word, the more you will be like Jesus.

When you look in the mirror, you are seeing Jesus – not yourself, but Jesus – letting Him shine out through your eyes, letting Him come out of your mouth, with the glory of God on your countenance, on your face. Let the glory of the Lord shine out of you.

I did a retreat at Sapulpa, Oklahoma, recently. A lady came in and I didn't know she was separated from her husband, and that just the previous Sunday she had given her heart to Jesus. She was forever changed by the ministry of the Holy Spirit. She danced before the Lord and then fell prostate in His manifested presence. As she arose from the floor the glory of God on her made her shine. We could have turned the lights off she was so full of His glory.

I believe in what Mary Kay says, that any old barn looks better with a little paint, so I use all the help I can get. But makeup will not do for you what the glory of the Lord will do. God wants you to know that you have been created in His image. You can accept yourself because you had nothing to do with being here on this earth.

Even if you were born out of wedlock, or you don't know who your mother and father are, God said, **"Before I formed you in the womb I knew and approved of you [as My chosen instrument], and before you were born I separated and set you apart, consecrating you . . ."** (Jeremiah 1:5). In other words, "I knew you before you were formed in the womb of your mother, and I charted every day of your life." So God knew. There are no mistakes in God's Kingdom. You have a divine appointment to be on this earth for such an hour as this.

So that should wipe out the statements: "I didn't know my mother, and I didn't know my daddy. I started out bad." Even if there was abuse as a child, when you come into the Kingdom of God, old things pass away, and all things become new. God will heal you, set you upright, and you will see yourself in the image of God. This should set you free.

Remember, I am the one who sat on my front porch and cried, "God, why did You make me like I am?"

Self-worth or Pride?

What is the difference between self-worth and pride? This is a distinction that is hard for some Christians to perceive. "Self-worth" is a conviction that you have a fundamental value because you were created by God in His image and because Jesus died for you. "Pride" always points to self. It is rooted in the pleasure that you find in yourself for what you believe that you can do or have done with your life. Pride is an attitude of superiority. It is a puffed-up mentality that manifests itself in an arrogant, unrealistic estimation of oneself in comparison with everyone else. Pride makes you think you are better than someone else.

The balance is humility, knowing who you are, who made the person you are, and giving glory to God. I am who I am by the grace of God. Look at Jesus! People were drawn to Him and the love of God in Him just like they are drawn to you, and the masses began to follow Him.

Jesus had crusades that had thousands of people in them, a congregation larger than I have ever preached to at one time. Yet, He never got so big that He couldn't take a towel, bend, and wash the disciples' feet. He had that spirit of humility upon Him. So we are not to get puffed up. In fact, we are called to be servants, and we need to remember that regarding our homes. We are called to be servants – to reach out our hands to the needy, not just outside the home, but in the home as well. It is a divine calling and a ministry.

Now, the devil will try to steal your self-image. Look at the story of Moses in Exodus 3:11. When God called him, he said, "Who, me?" He didn't think he could lead the children of Israel out of bondage and be their leader. But God anointed and appointed him.

God has anointed and appointed you to be in the position that you are in. That was dumb of the devil to do something like that. Can you believe that he tried to tempt Jesus in Matthew 3:17 KJV when Jesus was baptized and the Holy Spirit came announcing who He was? A loud voice came out of heaven, saying, **"This is my beloved Son, in whom I am well pleased."** In the very next chapter, Matthew 4:3 KJV, the devil said to Jesus, **"If thou be the Son of God, command that these stones be made bread."** He tempted Jesus to question who He was.

Let me tell you what the devil's favorite words are: "If you really were a Christian, you wouldn't act that way." "If you really were a good wife, you wouldn't have that attitude." He will always come and bring doubt about who you are. You just kick him out, saying, "Devil, I am a blood-bought, cleansed, righteous woman." Speak out who you are in Christ.

The key to having good self-esteem and not getting into pride is to understand the righteousness of God through Christ Jesus. "Righteousness" is simply defined as "right standing with God." It gives a person the ability to be free of guilt, condemnation, fear, and inferiority. These four problems rob many Christians of God's blessings. It is easy to see why an understanding of righteousness could transform a person's life. No guilt, no fear, no condemnation, and no inferiority. What a blessed life that would be!

Romans 5:17 KJV says:

> **For if by one man's offence death reigned by one; much more they which receive abundance of grace and the gift of righteousness shall reign in life by one, Jesus Christ.**

The gift of righteousness is wrapped up. We cannot do anything to become righteous. It is wrapped up like a gift – a gift of righteousness that Jesus has already paid for. Scripture says we shall reign in life by one, Jesus Christ. Reigning is winning. Jesus paid the price for our sin, for our unrighteousness. The human race owed a tremendous debt of sin and because man was unable to pay the debt, God sent His own Son to pay for it (1 Peter 2:24). Jesus was our substitute. He took our place, paying the awful price for sin. He did it because He loved us (John 3:16,17).

Now that the debt is paid, we are given a right standing with God. It is actually the right standing that Jesus earned as a result of His obedience unto death. We receive His righteousness the moment we take Jesus as our precious Lord and Savior.

> **For he hath made him to be sin for us, who knew no sin; that we might be made the righteousness of God in him.**
>
> 2 Corinthians 5:21 KJV

Christ dwells in our hearts. We have the righteousness of God, and we are made to be the righteousness of God in Him. His righteousness is for all who believe.

> **But now the righteousness of God without the law is manifested, being witnessed by the law and the prophets;**
> **Even the righteousness of God which is by faith of Jesus Christ unto all and *upon all them that believe:* for there is no difference:**
> **For all have sinned, and come short of the glory of God;**
> **Being justified freely by his grace through the redemption that is in Christ Jesus.**
>
> Romans 3:21-24 KJV

The message of righteousness is very good news. The moment we hear this word, it should cause faith to rise in our hearts. We want to receive it as ours – a gift from God – but we must *believe* and *confess* our sins, as Romans 10:10 KJV states:

> **For with the heart man *believeth* unto righteousness; and with the mouth *confession* is made unto salvation.**

So it is very important that we understand righteousness and what it means. ***Capsule:*** It means when I make a mistake that because Jesus has paid the price for my sins, He [Jesus] gets between me and the Father God, and when the Father looks at Janet Lay, He doesn't look at me as I am. He looks at me through Jesus, who is perfect. He doesn't see me as I am today. *He sees me as the finished product.* That means I can come boldly before the Father because Jesus is standing between me and the Father. He paid the price. That means I have no right to put down the daughter of God for whom the precious blood of Jesus was shed, and I can have right standing with the heavenly Father.

I pray that you will get hold of this truth. It will cause your old poor self-image, your old inferiority, and your old pity parties to cease. Once I got hold of this truth, it made me square my shoulders and straighten my back – one of the best adjustments you can get! You will know that you can walk and every place your feet touch you will be a blessing. You can walk in the blessings of God and you can talk about them. You are blessed in the home, in the field, in the city, in the grocery store, and you will be a blessing everywhere you go. You will be looking for someone to pour a blessing upon.

I say, "I am a blessing." It's not pride. It is knowing what Jesus has done for you. I have received the gift of righteousness that Jesus paid for.

I would be so disappointed if I shopped and shopped and spent the most money I had ever paid for a gift for someone, having it gift wrapped better than I could do it, then have the person for whom I purchased it say, "No, I don't want it. It's not for me." That would hurt my feelings. I would have to deal with my attitude for a long time. Every time I saw the person I would say, "That woman didn't know what a valuable gift I offered her."

Yet, some people have a lack of knowledge that we have right standing with God, and He wants us to reign as kings and queens in this life. It is so important to you today that you understand this teaching. Having a good image is an attitude rather than an attribute, and the makeover begins in the mind. We are not all going to have a size ten body, but we can be healthy and have a good mind.

> Jesus is saying to you today, "Righteousness is all wrapped up and paid for – the best gift you will ever receive!"

I want you to memorize Psalm 139:14 in *The Living Bible:*

Thank you for making me so wonderfully complex! It is amazing to think about. Your workmanship is marvelous – and how well I know it.

This will help you with your self-image. It is not mind over matter; it is Word over matter.

I memorized the following passage from Psalm 139:13-18 TLB, and it set me free:

You made all the delicate, inner parts of my body, and knit them together in my mother's womb.
Thank you for making me so wonderfully complex! It is amazing to think about. Your workmanship is marvelous – and how well I know it.
You were there while I was being formed in utter seclusion!
You saw me before I was born and scheduled each day of my life before I began to breathe. Every day was recorded in your Book!
How precious it is, Lord, to realize that you are thinking about me constantly! I can't even count how many times a day your thoughts turn towards me. And when I waken in the morning, you are still thinking of me!

Look in your mirror, and if you can't look squarely at the image yet, keep looking and begin to say, "Jesus loves you" and receive that love! (I couldn't look squarely at myself when I first started out. There were things in my life that I needed to repent of and get rid of.)

There will come a time when you will look in the mirror and say, "Jesus loves you, and I love you too!" It is okay to love yourself because you were purchased by the precious blood of Jesus. This is an assignment that sometimes women have a little difficulty with, but after I give you some scriptures that will produce faith for a good self-image, it will become easier.

Scriptures for a Good Self-Image

Here are several scriptures that will help to build your self-image. (Take the time to look up the actual scriptures.)

Philippians 4:7,8 - Think on these things.

2 Corinthians 5:17 - I created you a new creation. Old things are passed away, all things have become new.

Ephesians 2:10 - You are special.

Romans 5:5 - You are loved.

Romans 15:7 - You are accepted.

Colossians 2:10 - You are complete.

Galatians 3:13 - You are redeemed.

John 15:14 - You are valuable and precious. You are a friend of Jesus if you keep His commandments.

Isaiah 43:7-10 - You have a purpose in life.

Acts 1:8 - You have been given an assignment. Each person has something to do.

Psalm 145:14 - You are continually sustained by God and accompanied by Him.

Jeremiah 15:16 - You are God's responsibility. This is one of my favorites. When I blow it, I use this verse, saying, "Father, You have got to help me get out of it." He does because He loves me.

Psalm 8:4-6 - You are valuable to God and you have dominion. He made us a little lower than Himself, and He crowned us with glory and honor. That means He places value on us. Now, some of your Bibles say, "A little lower than angels," but if you check it out the word is "Elohim," and it means God. It should not be translated "angels."

Psalm 91 - You have security guards around you everywhere you go. You are so important. You know the President and others have their security guards. Psalm 91 tells me that the angels of the Lord are encamped round about me, so I have protection everywhere I go. The guards are around me everywhere I go. Natural security guards don't hold a candle to my security guards.

1 John 4:4 - You are of God, little children, and have overcome Satan because greater is He who is in you than he who is in the world.

1 John 5:4 - You are victorious over the world. This means you can have victory.

> Holy Spirit, seal the scriptural truths in this lesson in the minds of each reader.

Isaiah 49:15,16 - You are not forgotten. Verse 16 in the *King James Version* says, **"Behold, I have graven thee upon the palms of my hands; thy walls are continually before me."**

Acts 17:28 - You have energy through Christ. **"For in him we live, and move, and have our being . . ."** (KJV).

Philemon 6 - You are effective in every good thing. **"That the communication of thy faith may become effectual by the acknowledging of *every good thing which is in you* in Christ Jesus"** (KJV).

Nuggets from Chapter 2

In chapter 2, we taught on personal value and character. We taught on who you are in Christ Jesus, because if you notice in Proverbs 31:10, it starts out with who you are. It says, **"Who is he who can find her** [a virtuous woman]**? She is far more precious than jewels and her value is far above rubies or pearls."** It is important to know that you are valuable.

The first relationship is our relationship with God. Mark 12:29-31 KJV says:

> The first of all the commandments is, Hear, O Israel; The Lord our God is one Lord:
> And thou shalt love the Lord thy God with all thy heart, and with all thy soul, and with all thy mind, and with all thy strength: this is the first commandment.
> And the second is like, namely this, Thou shalt love *thy neighbour* as thyself. There is no other commandment greater than these.

So the first relationship is with God, but the second relationship is with yourself. If you do not feel good about yourself, you will have a hard time having healthy relations with other people. You are the channel that God's love flows through. A lot of times if you have poor self-esteem, you think you are not qualified and you don't have any abilities. You feel you have not been a success in life. If you don't accept who you are in Christ Jesus, then the love of God gets plugged up right there and it can't flow out to others.

We wonder why we have broken relationships. Many times it is because we don't feel good about ourselves so we cannot be that vessel from which the love of God flows. It might flow out some, but not as pure and good as it could if this vessel knows who he or she is in Christ.

A lot of people say, "Well, that is pride. You are not supposed to think more highly of yourself than you ought." We know the Scripture says that in Romans 12:3, but what are you thinking of yourself? You need to think of what God's Word says you are, not what someone says you were as a child, not what someone said because you are in a broken relationship, but what God says you are.

When you came to Jesus, He gave you the gift of righteousness. That means that you have right standing with our heavenly Father. That is the balance: You know who you are because of the price paid for you, which was the precious blood of Jesus. Accept that value! I do not believe God the Father, the Son, and the Holy Spirit made an investment in a "nobody."

> An investment was made in you, because you are valuable and precious, and God loves you.

When you come to Jesus, you trade all those old dirty rags of guilt, fear, inferiority, and condemnation of the past and you take on the robe of righteousness. I picture it in my mind as being a pure white robe, just like a bride wears down the aisle on her wedding day. It covers all your inadequacies. It covers all your weaknesses.

Now, when you have accepted the gift of righteousness, when the Father looks at you, He doesn't see all your weaknesses. Your past is under the blood of Jesus, and He sees you through Jesus. We know that Jesus is perfect. You can come boldly into the Father's throne room because Jesus is standing between you and the Father. He gave you right standing because of the price He paid.

When I had right standing with my earthly father, I loved to be in his presence. But when I did something I shouldn't have done, then I didn't want my daddy to scold me about it.

The good news is, because of what Jesus did, you can always have right standing with the Father. When you do something wrong, ask forgiveness, and it is cleansed and for-given. The Father sees you with right standing so you do not have to feel infe-rior. You do not have to have guilt. You do not have to have fear, because of what Jesus did. *Your part is to accept it.* This is what will help you have a good self-image.

> Righteousness is not some-thing you can earn. It comes because of what Jesus did when He died on the cross, took the keys of death and hell, rose from the dead, and ascended on high.

As a review, let's look at Second Corinthians 2:14 again:

But thanks be to God, Who in Christ always leads us in triumph [as trophies of Christ's victory] and through us spreads and makes evident *the fragrance of the knowledge of God* everywhere.

I hope you can begin to smell that sweet fragrance! I always like to emphasize this scripture because it is the goal or plan the Holy Spirit gave me for teaching Proverbs 31 and for the title of this course. The goal is to get a knowledge of the Word of God in our lives so we can be winners and smell sweet. We can become that sweet-smelling fragrance wherever we go and in whatever circumstances we face.

You can't get a fragrance off of the counter that will smell as good as the Word of God will in your life. If you know who you are in Christ Jesus, you are going to be a winner. You are a success looking for some-place to happen. A lot of people might say, "You are just a failure looking for a place to happen." No, you are a success looking for a place to happen.

In the Preface, I told you about the lady who could smell Christians. It is a good smell, not a bad smell. God gave this lady this gift, and I am sure it was to encourage her. She knew when a person was a Christian because she could smell that sweet aroma. She also was able to distinguish those who were stronger Christians than others. I wouldn't say they were better Christians, but maybe they had more of the knowledge of God in their lives, and that gave them a stronger, sweeter aroma. I don't know about you, but I want to be a sweet-smelling savor every place I go.

I am reminded of a lady who used to be my neighbor. When I traveled a lot, she cleaned my house a couple times a month. Our house was the only house she cleaned, and she was a wonderful housekeeper. One time when it was time for her to clean the house, her son Jeremy was not in school that day. They came to my home in Verdigris, Oklahoma, where we lived before moving to Grove, Oklahoma.

Jeremy said, "Mama, there is something that smells so good in Janet's house. Find out what it is." I love candles, and I am sure the candles had already been burning. Cindy said they went to every room and smelled every candle, but they couldn't find where the smell was coming from. (I have candles in about every room.) Cindy, a born-again, Spirit-filled believer, said the Holy Spirit said to her, "This is the aroma of the sweet fragrance of the knowledge that abides in this house."

When we were building our house, we had different ones who were not Christians who came out to the house, especially after we moved there and some things needed to be finished. I remember a man who came out on business who brought his wife. He walked through our house and he kept saying that our house smelled so good. I knew what it was. It wasn't candles! It was the knowledge of God and the love of God that were in our home. It was the fragrance they could smell.

Don't you want your home to smell like that? When people walk in your house, they will smell the aroma of the sweet fragrance of God, discernible like Christians.

I am telling you, you have a beautiful opportunity to become a sweet-smelling fragrance. You need to know that is what you are, that wherever you go, shopping or to the grocery store, you become a sweet fragrance discernible alike among those who are perishing and among those who are not. That is what this book is about. I want to pour the knowledge of God's Word into your life and create such a desire in you that you will want that *sweet aroma of the knowledge of God!*

CHAPTER 3

Accepting and Understanding the Man

> The heart of her husband trusts in her confidently and relies on and believes in her securely, so that he has no lack of [honest] gain or need of [dishonest] spoil.
>
> She comforts, encourages, and does him only good as long as there is life within her.
>
> Proverbs 31:11,12

I realize that some single women may be reading this book. It is very important that you, as well as married women, have knowledge of acceptance and understanding of the male species. There are so-called "family programs" on television where the male is very put down, made fun of, and made to look like a wimp. God created man, and He did not create wimps. God put the man on this earth, and he is a special creature with the breath of God breathed into him. Man was put here for a reason.

No woman who has knowledge and understanding of man should ever be caught putting a man down. I did not say he does everything right. It is not our place to line them up, yet I know women are fixers and start trying to fix them the day of the marriage. I did.

I planned on changing Bill, but as you hear the story, you will hear me say that about the time I got him in my preconceived mold of what a perfect mate would be, out would come a leg. He just never did quite fit the mold. But you know what? He is a better guy today. The Holy Spirit did more for him in ten minutes than I did in twenty years. And so, if you would just love them and let God do the fixing, you will find out that God can work things out. Even if you are single, you need to know that you should let God change the man you might fall in love with.

If you are raising little boys, you will see these needs being manifested in their life as they continue to grow. I raised four sons, and I know they didn't just develop these needs when they got married. They had them while growing up.

So the lesson in this chapter is acceptance and understanding the man. I think this portion of Scripture is interesting because right after it talks about women, it talks about our husbands. It does not talk about your children as number one. If you will go back and look in the Word of God, you will find that your first responsibility is to your husband. That is the way God made it.

> Accepting a man does not mean to be blind to his mistakes. The answer is to look for the best in him and allow for mistakes.

Now, God wants your children raised and your husbands want them taken care of, but in your attitude, *husbands want to be the number one person in your life.* Not your number one relationship – that is with God. There is no competition between the relationship with God and the relationship with your husband. You can only love your husband like you should if you have a right relationship with God because He is the One who instructs you.

Perfect mates only come in gloves and shoes. There are no perfect mates, or perfect husbands, but caring wives accept them as God's gift to them. God did not give you a man to fix. All good and perfect gifts come from God. He gave him to you to love, not to fix.

I think it is interesting that in Genesis 2:18 God made the beautiful garden and built a beautiful home for Adam and Eve to live in. The Bible does not say that it was a house. But it was beautiful – the most gorgeous place that has ever been put on this earth. All the animals were created. Everything was taken care of before they brought woman on the scene.

God and Adam sat down, and they named everything in order. I wondered why they didn't wait for me to get on the scene to help them with that! I know if I had been on the scene, I probably would have changed everything they did. I would have said, "Now you know that is not a skunk; it looks like a rabbit. We'd better change the squirrel to a skunk." I would have wanted to rename everything and fix it all up – LIKE WE DO WITH OUR HUSBANDS WHEN WE GET MARRIED!

I remember when Bill and I were first married, he tried to help me do everything. I remember his first day off. When I returned from work, he had cleaned our little apartment. It was really small. Only one person could get in the kitchen. We had a little folding table against the wall, and the bed came out of the wall. It was too small for you to use the restroom and take a shower at the same time. I mean, it was tiny! Bill had cleaned the apartment and was trying to do the ironing. Twenty years later he didn't do anything, and I wondered why.

As I began to examine my life, I realized that anything he did, I did it right behind him. He did not do it good enough. He never could wipe the cabinet off good enough. Even today if I am not careful, I will go behind him and redo the things he does. Husbands can't please us at times, so we redo, correct, or try to do better than what they have done.

Men don't have the same perception of things as we do. That really came home to me one day when we got home from church. We had begun to put things together, and we had been married over twenty years. Bill came in and said, "What can I help you do?" I was getting lunch ready, and I said, "Well, if you can't see what there is to do, just forget it." So he went into the living room, turned on the football game, and forgot it.

I thought, *I can't believe that you don't know to put the silverware on the table and you can't see that the salad needs to be cut up.* The Holy Spirit spoke to me, "If you went to work with him on Monday morning, would you know the first thing to do on his job?"

The Holy Spirit and my husband allowed me to work for a month at the newspaper company where he worked. I want to tell you, when I saw how the women he supervised treated him, my actions got shaped up a lot quicker because they treated him with respect. When he came into the room, all heads raised up and it was, "What can I do for you, Mr. Lay?" "Do you need something, Mr. Lay?" "Did I do this right, Mr. Lay?" There was none of that, "Do it yourself." They treated him with respect. So I think it would behoove all of us to recognize the gift that God has given us and shape up. You love him and let God shape him up. So we need to accept God's gift to us.

Why is it important for a man to be himself and do his own thing? Well, maybe it is because everyone should be able to develop their own ability. That's true. Maybe it's that he is a rebel and has to have things his own way. Have you ever felt that? No, the answer to that is when he is always trying to please others, it does not allow him to listen to the Holy Spirit.

When I teach these things and point a finger, I have four fingers coming back to me. I am convinced that a lot of times they cannot hear God because all they hear is our voice trying to tell them what to do, what God is doing, and what God is speaking. I'll teach on it later, but in First Peter 1:7 it talks about a quiet and peaceful spirit that is very precious in the sight of God. If you look up the meaning of "precious," it is only mentioned two other times in the New Testament. One is describing the precious blood of Jesus, the other is like precious faith.

> I am convinced that men could hear from God a lot easier if wives would get out of their ear.

52

A quiet and peaceful spirit in a woman does not talk, talk, talk. I know I am a talker, but we need to learn that there are times to be quiet and pray for our husbands. If we never allow them to hear from the Holy Spirit, who is trying to speak to them, giving them direction, and all they ever hear is from us, that doesn't allow them to grow spiritually. So it is very important that we allow him to be himself and let God speak to him about things.

I found out when I began to let the Holy Spirit speak to my husband and let him do some things his way, I was amazed at his wisdom. I only share these things, not to uncover, but to let you know that I have not always been a bad person, but some of the things I did were really bad. I remember having an attitude toward my husband that I was much wiser than he. Yet, when I began to get my eyes opened and do things right and began to see the Word of God, I realized that my husband was the foreman over 300 people on his job. He ran the production of the newspaper in Tulsa and had all these employees under him. Yet, I thought I was the only one with all the wisdom. So it is important for him to be himself and to do things in the manner for which he has the talent and ability to do them.

A Man Needs Respect and Reverence

Understanding a man is to know his need for respect and reverence. Let's look to Ephesians 5, verse 33, which happens to be my husband's favorite scripture:

> However, let each man of you [without exception] love his wife as [being in a sense] his very own self; and let the wife see that she *respects* and *reverences* her husband [that she notices him, regards him, honors him, prefers him, venerates, and esteems him; and that she defers to him, praises him, and loves and admires him exceedingly].

I remember when I first heard this scripture. It was at a retreat where a lady was teaching on marriage after the main service. I did not know about *The Amplified Bible* and when they said *Amplified Bible,*

I thought, *What's that?* I only knew about one Bible – the *King James.* And this lady didn't teach really. She just shared a little and said this scripture will tell you exactly the need in understanding a man and to know his need.

Now, to understand the man, you must know that he needs your respect and he needs your trust. You might say, "But I cannot trust him." Well, are you praying for him? Can you trust God? If you can trust God to line your husband up, you don't have to do it. If you are praying for your husband, the Bible says the prayers of a righteous person availeth much. If you are washing him with the Word of God on a daily basis, the Holy Spirit will go after him like the bloodhound of heaven and see that he hears from God each day.

The Amplified Bible says you are to *respect* your husband and to *notice* him. After they get married, a lot of women forget to notice their husband. They think he is a big boy now. He can take care of himself.

I had an attitude. Attitudes are stinky sometimes. I had four children to care for and thought that since my husband was a big boy, he could take care of himself because I was busy with the children. Children grow up, leave, and they are gone. And here is a husband who sometimes works eight to ten hours a day, sometimes one job, sometimes two, and no one notices when he comes in.

When Bill and I nearly lost our marriage, he left. And when he came back and we began to talk about things, he said, "Well, I didn't think you even cared whether I came home or not, if I just brought my paycheck home on Friday." I do not think I am the only woman in the world who has ever done that.

I am saying to you, Come on, he needs to be noticed. He needs to be noticed when he is tired. Sometimes he needs an extra kiss on his forehead when he is sitting in his chair. It is not up to you to keep him humble. It is up to you to build him up. The world will keep him humble because it is a hard place out there where he has to go.

So the Bible says you are to *respect* your husband. It goes on to say that you need to *regard* him. You *regard* him in his decisions, feelings, visions, and goals. This does not mean that you have to ask him if he wants beans for supper every evening or ask him about trivial things, but you regard him. You try to cook the things you know he likes – those little special things. Scripture says she will comfort, encourage, and do him only good as long as there is life within her. That should be a goal. It doesn't say you do that if you want to. The Word from the Lord says that you do it regardless of what kind of husband you have. You are to *honor* him. This means to *place value* upon him.

You are to *prefer* him. Now, let me tell you. I know that girlfriends are wonderful, lady friends are precious, and children are special, but the one you are to prefer above everyone else is your husband. You say, "I just haven't got to that state." You just keep working at it.

My husband is my best friend. I have a lot of friends, but if I have extra moments to spend, the person I want to spend them with is my husband. I love being with my husband. I haven't always felt that way. But I prefer him over any other situation or relationship.

So Scripture says she prefers him. She venerates and esteems him. She *defers* to him. She gives in. She submits to him. She says, "Okay, Honey, if you want to eat at Charlie's Chicken today, that is all right with me." She may really want Mexican food. There is a balance to these things. I am just giving you an example, but she defers to him.

She *praises* him. That means you give him compliments on a daily basis. Don't let someone else give your husband those words of praise. I am telling you that just the time you start neglecting that, the enemy will have the cutest little gal sitting someplace, maybe a coffee shop, who will tell him how good he smells or how good he looks. She will say, "Man, you are getting younger. I can't believe the age that you are. You look younger every day." You had better be sure that he gets those praises from you and not from someone else. If you fill him up with praise, there will not be a place for someone else to give it to him.

You know what? Lots of women in the church have blessed my husband with complimenting him on his messages or whatever, but let me tell you. Before we get home from every service, I tell him how good he preaches. I say, "Wow! You did a good job today. That was great!"

Do you hear what I am saying to you? You be the one who praises your husband and do not let someone else give him all the words of praise. *The Amplified Bible* says, "She loves and admires him." You need to admire him as a husband. You need to admire him as a lover, telling him he is a good lover. You need to admire his appearance, accomplishments, skills, and character. You admire him and give him those words of admiration.

Appreciate His Masculinity

Understanding a man is knowing his need for appreciation of his masculinity.

Your husband needs your respect and trust. However a man may appear, his nature is basically insecure. Often a man's masculinity is more fragile than a woman's femininity. His *self-esteem* is more easily threatened. Men more than women need to prove themselves.

I remember when our two older sons were planning to get married. We were making a move at that time to our new home in Verdigris, Oklahoma. So on this particular Sunday afternoon all of our things were packed as we were making the move. Mike and Tom were dating Debby and Pam. Pam and Tom were already engaged. Mike and Debby had only been dating about sixty days. The boys still lived at home at that time. We decided to have a cookout after church, so we took our hamburgers to the park as our house was in an upheaval and we couldn't fix lunch at home.

Mike and Tom started having a little wrestling match, but what started out as a wrestling match ended up being a full-fledged battle. Now, why would they do that since they weren't mad at each other? I'll tell you why. Because Debby and Pam were looking on, and they had to prove who was the strongest. Mom and Dad had to get in the middle and separate two brothers who weren't mad at each other but were about to kill each other. After they became adults, we didn't allow them to get into too many wrestling matches. Men simply have to prove themselves.

So I am telling you, men have a need to prove themselves. It's very important for doubts are always lingering regarding their manhood. The view a man has of himself, whether good or bad, is usually reflected from two sources – his work and his woman. If either of these become shaky, so do his feelings – his perception about his manhood. He even feels depression and anger at such times.

A wife's ongoing responsiveness to her husband should be a well from which a husband can draw respect for himself. His respect is in many ways her respect reborn in him. Do you hear it? Her respect. So if you do not respect your husband, if you put him down, if you are trying to control him and be his mother or his Holy Spirit, and you don't allow him to prove he has talents and abilities, then you will find that he is very angry.

Many times a man will become depressed and very critical. It wouldn't make any difference if you cooked the best dinner and had the table set just right with the candles on it and the house spotless. If you have been putting him down, he is going to criticize what you are doing. Why? He doesn't feel good about himself because he hasn't been built up. You haven't been giving him those words of appreciation.

When you find a man who is harsh and critical and resentful, either the job situation is hard or he's got a wife who is not respecting him or responding to him at home. Now I know that is not always the reason, but it is the major thing. I know because I have counseled a lot and I have watched it too many times. When you have a man acting that way, I am telling you, there is something hurting on the inside. God has given you the ability to build him up and cause him to come out of that mode. It's your respect reborn in him.

Few areas affect a man as much as having a wife who is responsive to him. Spontaneous hugs and kisses and other demonstrations of affection, as well as lovemaking, all do more than just give pleasure. These things reassure a man and confirm his masculinity.

God is the One who thought up sex, and He says it is good. If God says it is good, then we should be a participant in it. Hebrews 13:4 KJV says the marriage bed is undefiled. The same Bible that tells you not to lie and steal also tells you not to defraud your husband. Now, I am not talking about fifteen times a day, but I am saying that you should take care of your husband. If you are turned off, you need to get in the bathroom at night and get ready for your lover. Smell good, look good, and go to bed with your husband.

A lot of women have called me and said, "I hate sex." It hasn't been just two or three. They say, "I don't like it. I don't want it." I tell them, "You get in the bathroom tonight, get yourself ready, and crawl into bed ready to minister to him."

> Your husband needs reverence, respect, and sex.

You know what? They call me back and say it was the best time for them. You cannot give without receiving. I am just saying to you, I am a woman, an older woman, and the Word of God tells me in Titus 2:4,5 that I am to teach younger women to love their husbands. And you need to love your husbands in the bedroom. If you defraud your husband and you don't have a good sexual relationship, it would be like going to church and all you would hear would be preaching with no praise and worship.

Get busy! Go and buy you something alluring and sweet smelling. [3] And don't forget spontaneous hugs. Few areas affirm a man as much as his wife's sexual responsiveness.

---

[3] It has been said that Billie, wife of Zigfield, whose business was beautiful women, arose an hour earlier than he did each morning and made herself a radiant beauty. Esther in the Old Testament, like Billie, did not approach the king until she looked like Miss Universe. She got the right smell, she got the right eye appeal, and then she said, "If I perish, I perish!" The king took one look at her and broke all the laws of the kingdom!

Minister to him with spontaneous hugs and other demonstrations of affection as well as lovemaking. This will do more than just give him pleasure. These things reassure a man and confirm his masculinity. A respectful wife is life-giving to a man. He draws from her a strong and affirmative sense of who he is. Truly, a wife can brighten her husband's life by her admiration and esteem of him.

She can stabilize his life by her supportiveness. She can also energize his life by her physical responsiveness. She is called to fulfill many of his deepest needs through the simple admonition, see to it that you respect your husband. Other than a man's relationship with the Lord, few things tell a man more about himself than does the respect of his wife.

Ways To Bring Shame to Husbands

One way to bring shame to husbands is to always have the answer.[4] Spending too much money could also do it. But the main way she brings shame to him is through envy, jealousy, and wrath. There is nothing worse than a jealous wife who is always checking out every place her husband has been and what he has done. I realize there are some husbands who give their wives reasons for jealousy; however, jealousy is a sin. I tell you, envy, jealousy, and wrath (anger) have destroyed more people.[5]

I have seen more situations where a woman is insecure because she doesn't feel good about herself. You need to know that you are God's gift to your husband. The best thing that ever happened to him was when he married you. This is why I taught on self-esteem first. You are his gift from God. Even if you have had a situation where a husband has been unfaithful, you need to forgive and go on because you are constantly picking on the place where he has been unfaithful or what

---

[4] Proverbs 12:4 KJV - "A virtuous woman is a crown to her husband: but she that maketh ashamed is as rottenness in his bones."
[5] Proverbs 14:30 KJV - "A sound heart is the life of the flesh: but envy the rottenness of the bones."

he has done wrong. As long as you pick something, it is going to stay sore. *You have to forgive by faith, not by feelings.* It is very important that you begin to build that confidence and not be jealous, for jealousy will destroy a relationship.

My husband has never given me any reason to be jealous. However, because of my insecurity I was jealous of him. I used to have him timed from work to home, and he had better not be a minute late or I wanted to know what turn he took, etc. I had him timed from the newspaper company to our house. So I am not telling you something that I have not experienced.

And let me tell you something. Jealousy does not come from God, but from the devil to destroy you and your relationship. As far as I know, and I believe it is true, my husband from the day he married me has never been unfaithful to me. He has no reason to be treated that way. It had to do with control and insecurity.

> "And ye shall know the truth, and the truth shall make you free"
>
> (John 8:32 kjv).

If you are having a problem with jealousy, you need to start trusting God to take care of your husband and treat him so good that he will be home a minute early instead of a minute late. It takes time to undo things.

If he doesn't come home on time, you might check out why he doesn't want to come home. Is the atmosphere good? Can he come home to a wife who is glad to see him? Do you have the candles burning? Can he smell good food when he walks in the door? Is the bed unmade and the clutter so high that he can't get through? Are the kids screaming and yelling? That is not the way to set your house for your husband to come home. We will talk about that later when we talk about organization. But let me tell you, he needs to know he is trusted and that there is no envy or jealousy.

I used to tell my husband (I hope you will love me after reading all this), "I wish you would stay home for a day and do the housework and let me go to the office." That is envy. I used to think his job would be a lot easier than my job. I worked with him one month and found out that his job was not easy.

Let me get back to my house, inside my four walls. I know what it is to have four children. I used to think they didn't know any word but "Mama." You can't even go in the bathroom and sit down without someone knocking on the door, saying, "Mama, Mama." Don't they know anything but "Mama"? But they do and the day will come when they will grow up and be gone. God has given you the blessing of being there at home with them now.

Check your attitude. A good attitude starts with gratitude. It will make you happy as I can testify. If your attitude is right, the work you have to do will not be as hard.

Why Do Women Try To Change Men?

This is a good question. I know you probably have not been guilty of it, but all of us have the preconceived idea of what the ideal mate will be.

I told you I had preconceived ideas of the way Bill was going to be as my mate. Not only that, I had a wonderful father. My father was phlegmatic, very quiet and easy going, and my sisters and I had him on a pedestal. My mother was strong and aggressive.

I didn't appreciate my mother until after I got married when I realized she was the one who had done all the discipline. But my very wise mother said to me one time when I was telling her how great Daddy was, "Honey, the only difference in your daddy and your husband is that you weren't married to your father." He wasn't my husband; he was my daddy. So I had a preconceived idea that Bill was going to do everything that my daddy did.

I never saw any of Daddy's faults. Daddy was just perfect – a perfect man. No, that was fantasy. My husband has just as many good qualities and he is stronger in some areas than Daddy was. It was a preconceived idea I had of how I wanted my husband to be. When I tried to change him into the image of someone else instead of allowing him to be in the image of God, I started trying to be like God.

Do not try to change your mate. You pray for him if he is in sin, but God created him in His image. Let him be the image God created him to be. They all have strengths and they all have weaknesses, but so do you. When you get into conflict, *it is one person's weakness rubbing against the other person's weakness.* I am not talking about physical abuse. I am talking about accepting your husband as a gift from God. So don't try to change him with your preconceived ideas.

I am reminded of the woman who went to divorce court one day. The judge looked at her husband and said, "What do you think the problem is? Why do you want a divorce?" The husband said, "Well, I really don't know. She changed the place we lived and changed the way I wore my clothes." (I tried to do that to Bill. I bought him bright clothes, bright shirts and ties. I tried to dress him just like me – rhinestones on his collar. He wouldn't wear them.)

> Just like you as a woman never get too old to be treated like a sweetheart, men never get too old to be admired. They need you to admire what they do.

The husband standing before the judge continued, "She changed the friends we had, she put me on a better eating plan and wouldn't let me have pork chops anymore. And now she says I am not the man she married."

Why do we try to change men? We think it is for their own good, or we say it is to glorify God. That's a holy one, isn't it? No, we try to change them because we have a preconceived idea of what they should be.

Paul writes in Ephesians 5:33 and we have already read it, that a woman should admire her husband. That means you ought to give him at least one compliment daily. And once a week you should give him a new compliment, something you have never said before.

If they are retired and at home, they need you to admire them for the little things they do. So you be the one who admires your husband. Whatever your husband does, you look for ways to admire him. If you will pray, the Holy Spirit will show you how to admire your husband.

Your next assignment is to *list ten good things about your husband.* You need to think of things you can admire. Think back to when you were attracted to him. You surely didn't find the man who could make you the most miserable in life and marry him. There surely was something that attracted you to that man. And even if you had to get married because you were pregnant, you surely didn't get pregnant by someone who didn't have something good about him. I know some mistakes have been made, but even in those mistakes, you did not find the person who made you miserable.

If you are not married, be sure that the person you find has the qualities that you can live with the rest of your life because you have no guarantee that anyone is going to change after they get married. In fact, most do not. So think about him. Think about what attracted you. I remember the good things about my husband. When I start thinking about my husband, it makes me want to go where he is and spend time with him.

How Does a Woman Wound a Man's Pride?

You can wound a man's pride by always having the answer, by always correcting him, and giving him dirty looks of disapproval, letting him know he can never do anything right. You can do things better than he can. You are always firing darts at him and it wounds his masculine pride. That is putting him down.

When I learned how wrong I was and started putting into practice the right way, I had twenty years of undoing a lot of things. But I remember the first time Bill and I went shopping for a new suit together. (I had bought all of his clothes and brought them home. I had toned them down because he wouldn't wear the bright ones.) Bill does not like to shop. He would send me on a preliminary trip, and I would pick things out. I had been to the store and picked out two or three suits, but I decided I wasn't going to take control of his shopping anymore.

When we went to this men's store in Tulsa, a gentleman walked up to us and said, "May I help you?" I didn't say anything. We stood there like we needed to use sign language. I just stood there, and Bill just stood there. I looked at him, and he looked at me. At last Bill said, "We would like to look at a suit." The man said, "What size?" I stood there. Bill looked at me. I looked at him and didn't say anything. He said, "I think it is a 40 or 42," so we headed back to the rack.

I had been in the day before. The man began to go through the rack and show Bill the suits. Finally, I told him that I had looked at two particular ones. I told the salesman what I was doing, because he looked at us like we were something strange. You know what the salesman said to me (at that time I was taking the class), "Where is that class? I want to send my wife to it."

Husbands don't want us always to have the answer. They don't want us always to take control.

I remember when I quit interrupting the stories my husband would tell. He would start to tell a story and when he would get to a certain point, I took it from there and finished it for him. I remember when I quit doing that, he would get to that point and wait for me to take over. I am not telling you things that are not true. It was liberating for him when I began to keep my mouth shut and not take the storytelling away from him and also not to correct him in public.

As Bill would start to tell a story and say it was Tuesday of last week, I would say, "Oh no, Honey. It was Wednesday of last week at three o'clock. Remember?" Well, who cared whether it was Tuesday or Wednesday? He was just trying to tell the story. Unless it was a point of information that would cause a problem, why correct him? No one really cares whether the roses are red or pink. Let them tell their story. Quit correcting them.

So how do you wound his pride? *By always correcting him, always having the answer, always finishing his stories, putting him down by saying, "My old man can't do anything right. His mother must never have taught him anything."* Those things wound his pride.

Also, you can wound him by your attitude. Let me give you another example. Several years ago, my husband traveled and was only home on weekends. There was an attitude at our house, never a spoken attitude, that when Daddy's home, there are certain things we can't do. When Daddy leaves, there are certain things we get to do because Daddy was stricter in his discipline.

So Saturday and Sunday the boys and I cleaned our act up. Monday morning we did our own thing. When I started getting my life in order, I went to my boys and apologized. That attitude was wrong because I needed their daddy. When they started getting taller than me, I needed their daddy to be there. And Bill always supported me. Even if I was wrong, he would support me in my decisions and then he would talk to me about it later. A house divided will not stand.[6]

As you teach your children, teach them respect for their father. Do not make them feel that he's too strict or give them a negative attitude toward his authority, for it will weaken his position in the family. God appointed him to be the head of the household. He didn't ask for it. God appointed him for it. So be careful of your attitude in your household about your husband and what attitude you put in your children.

How Do We Build His Self-image?

You can build your husband's self-image by complimenting him in the things I have shared with you. What happens when a man's pride has been wounded? He will be angry, or he will be depressed. Many times he will withdraw and not talk. Have you noticed that a man

---

[6]Mark 3:25 KJV - **"And if a house be divided against itself, that house cannot stand."**

quits talking when he gets married? Well, it could be that he cannot get a word in edgewise. It could be that you have not learned to listen.

Bill and I started out having a five-minute repeat back. He said it wasn't fair, because I can say more in five minutes than he can. But I listened to him intently for five minutes and didn't let my mind run ahead to what I was going to answer. Then I had to repeat back to him what he said. And sometimes when I repeated back he would say, "No, that is not what I meant. Let me try again." And he would share it again. He didn't say negative things to me, and I didn't say negative things to him. *We learned to communicate.*

You need to learn to listen to your husband when he talks. God gave you two ears and one mouth. That should tell you something. You should be listening twice as much as you are talking.

What is the struggle that goes on inside of them?

Husbands do not like to have conflict or confrontation, yet they want to be the leader so they feel pulled all the time and struggle because God put into man the ability to be the leader in the home.

What can you do to help him overcome the struggle?

You can release him. You can begin to compliment him. Allow him to finish his stories. Allow him to have some things his way.

Another place where I think women sometimes get into conflict is when you ride with your husband in the car and you correct him on his driving. We have a golden rule at our house: *Whoever drives, the other person does not say anything.* Sometimes you have to look out the window, especially if your husband drives a little high-powered El Camino and when he gets into your car, he wants to drive like it's the El Camino. Sometimes I say, "The Cadillac is saying it is not an El Camino."

There were two ways to go to church from where we lived, and I can guarantee you that Bill would take one direction and I would take the other. We would joke sometimes and say, "I wish you would go to church the right way like I do." But what difference does it make?

Do not be critical and always have to be in control. Don't give him directions all the time. Allow him to begin to do things his way and let him take back the control.

The most important things that a woman needs in the marriage are *love, security,* and *romance.* I am not writing or teaching to men right now, but men need to know birthdays are important with little gifts. I told my husband one time when we were beginning to get things right, "Honey, I don't care if you just bring me a gumball. It is not the gumball. It's the fact that you thought about me." I want to be his sweetheart from now on, and he has been bringing me lots of gumballs since then. But little things are important to women, and men think those things are so foolish.

Anniversaries are important to women. Our son, Tom, said when he and Pam first got married, "I'll be so glad when our first year anniversary gets here. I have to remember every week the certain time we got married. It's been one week, two weeks, then four weeks, now it has been a month. We are now on the second month. I'll be glad when we get to the year because I am having a hard time with all these anniversaries the first year."

It is not wrong for you to want your husband to remember, but you need to understand that those things are not as important to him. They have to learn these things also. Bill thought these things were so foolish and he was shocked when we began to teach marriage and the family. He tells the men, "Little things are important to women – those anniversaries, the dates, the car door."

The first time Bill began opening the car door for me again, I remember we had gone into this music store in Tulsa, Oklahoma, and when we came out, Bill went to my side of the car and I went to his side of the car. He said, "I really didn't want you to drive. I was just going to open the door for you." I had to learn to let him do those things for me again.

When our sons became young men, they would get after me when we went to shopping malls and I would reach out to open the door. They would say, "Mom, let me open the door for you." Men need you to let them do that. Step back and wait.

I remember a pastor's wife who played the piano for their church. She and her husband got to church early one Sunday. We had been teaching about opening car doors and those courtesies. So he went on into the church and was getting ready for the service, but soon he realized that his wife was not in the sanctuary. He kept looking for her and pretty soon someone noticed that she was still sitting in the car. He went out and said, "What's wrong, Honey? Are you sick or something?" She said, "No, I'm waiting for you to open the car door."

You may need to stay in the car. They may walk off and leave you, but they will get the point. When you were dating they opened your door.

Let's talk about where you sit in the car. Your husband never moved from driving the car. You moved over next to the door where you are almost falling out. You need to move over a little and be close to him and touch him.

When we go driving together, many times I reach over and touch his hand. He's my sweetheart, he's my lover, he's my husband, and I touch him. And I'm not ashamed to do that because he is the gift that God has given me. But sometimes we can forget how important these things are.

So what are the most important things a woman has in marriage? *Love, security, and romance.* What are the most important things a man has need of? *Respect, reverence, and sex.*

Before you read the next chapter, I want you to take some 3 x 5 cards, you can get decorative with them if you like, and write the word "LOOK" on them. I want you to place them several places in your home. Don't tell your husband or family what these are for. They are to remind you to look to their better side. It will help you with your children also. If you put one on the telephone, it will help to remind you to look at a person's better side when they call you. Keep that a secret until the end of the book.

I know one husband who ripped them down because his wife wouldn't tell him what the cards were for. She then told him, "Honey, those were to remind me to look to your better side." Mine was appliqued. Someone appliqued it and put it in a little embroidery hoop. They had appliqued the word "look" on it, put eye lashes on the two o's to make them eyes. It was real cute and I enjoying using it as I was learning to look for good qualities in Bill. *Be creative.*

In my own life, I found myself to be a very critical person. I would always look at people negatively – what they needed to change, or what they needed to do. My husband worked nights at the newspaper office in Tulsa for many years, and I would go to pick him up or take him to work. I would have opportunities to park in downtown Tulsa in regard to his job. So I would sit in the car and look at people as they walked down the street.

I would think, *She needs to lose weight. Wow! Wonder when was the last time she was at a hairdresser.* All of us have had bad hair days, but I was very critical. *I wonder how he got her.* I would think things like that, never looking at the value of a person.

When I put up my "look" signs and began to look for the positive in people, it really helped me in relationships because every person is valuable and precious. And who are we to judge another person? The Scripture says, **"Judge not, that ye be not judged"** (Matthew 7:1 KJV). When you put someone else down, you are putting down one of God's creations, and you have God to answer to regarding your critical spirit.

Nuggets from Chapter 3

Chapter 3 was about accepting and understanding the man.

There is no competition between your relationship with God and the relationship with your husband. You can love your husband like you should only if you have a right relationship with God, because He is the One who instructs you.

There are no perfect mates or perfect husbands. Caring wives accept them as God's gift to them.

A lot of men cannot hear from God because all they hear is your voice trying to tell them what to do or what God is speaking to them.

> Accepting a man does not mean to be blind to his mistakes. The answer is to look for the best in him and allow for mistakes.

The husband needs reverence, respect, and sex.

Just as a woman never gets too old to be treated like a sweetheart, men never get too old to be admired and to be the head of the household as God intended.

CHAPTER
4

Understanding the Pressures of the Man

As a review, in chapter 2, you were to write twenty good things about yourself. In chapter 3, you were to write ten good things about your husband. You were also asked to make some "look" cards to place in your house to remind you to look to your husband's good points, as well as those of other people. In the last chapter, we discussed accepting and understanding the man. We were also discussing how we tend to be critical of others, which is the reason to make the "look" cards.

Women tend to be fixers. I try hard not to be a fixer, but I want to fix everything and make it better. My little daughter-in-law had some things left from the Arts and Crafts Show, and I just wanted to buy it all from her because she was going to have to take the things not sold back home with her. I wanted to fix it for her. So we tend to be fixers and sometimes we get critical with our fixing.

We look to negative things and we think, *This is the way it should be.* Your "look" signs will help you look at the good things in life and not the negative. I believe God wants us to do that. Our eyes are the windows of our soul, and when we are always looking in a negative mode, we speak in a negative mode. We are going to be gossiping, we are going to be critical, and we are going to be putting other people down.

Your assignment in this chapter (and you single ladies are going to get off unless you have a family member you dare ask), I want you to ask your husband for three things he would like for you to change. Only three. You tell him, "Only three."

Identifying Men's Pressure Sources

Man's first pressure is from God. After man sinned in the garden of Eden, God gave him this word:

> **And to Adam He said, Because you have listened and given heed to the voice of your wife and have eaten of the tree of which I commanded you, saying, You shall not eat of it, the ground is under a curse because of you; in sorrow and toil shall you eat [of the fruits] of it all the days of your life.**

Genesis 3:17

You might say, "I thought we were redeemed from the curse of the law" (Galatians 3:13). That is true, but this judgment was given to man before the curse of the law and it is still in effect.[7] I believe that even if a man is not a Christian, he still feels this pressure because it is inherent in his nature. There is a knowing in a man that when he marries, he is responsible for his wife and family.

If the man is a Christian, he knows as the head of the household he is responsible for the spiritual condition of his family. First Corinthians 11:3 states, **"But I want you to know and realize that Christ is the Head of every man, the head of a woman is her husband, and the Head of Christ is God."**

Man's second pressure is financial.

---

[7] 1 Timothy 5:8 KJV - "But if any provide not for his own, and specially for those of his own house, he hath denied the faith, and is worse than an infidel."

He wants to be confident that his wife and children will be provided for if he should die or become disabled. He wants to make sure that his children have an opportunity for a good education so that they will have good lives. Finally, he wants to know that he will have a retirement so that he and his family can enjoy their latter years.

Man's third pressure is position and status in the workforce and in the family.

In the world that we live in, there are many demands and there is little security. I have seen men who worked on jobs for years and all of a sudden they get the pink slip in the box. As a man trying to make a living for his family and be a success on his job or in his profession, the insecurity that is in the world today makes it very difficult.

I realize that there may be singles reading this book, and there are exceptions to the rule. I have had several jobs in my adult life, and when I got tired of a job, I could quit. But my husband has never had the option of quitting. I am trying to make the point that husbands always have the responsibility of making a living for the family because of the role God ordained for the man.

> Nothing is really secure except your relationship with Jesus Christ.

There are men who are independent workers, but they are up at 8:00 a.m. looking for work to make a living. Our neighbor said that he didn't know pastors went to work at 8:00 a.m., but my husband did. He considered that pastoring the church was his employment and also that he was making the living for both of us.

So, the pressures and demands in the world today bring little security, and men really worry about whether they will be able to provide for their families. They worry about the success on their jobs. They worry about the education of their children since colleges cost so much. Will there be money to put their children through school? They are concerned for not only their future, but also for the future of their family.

In striving for status, a husband may lose rather than win the position. Many times men go up the ladder for a while and someone comes in who has been working for maybe a year and that person goes up the ladder ahead of him. That can be very discouraging.

The other thing I think is that as men get older, they are not able to do some of the things they were able to do as younger men.[8] So they are constantly having this turmoil – the emotion of their position and their status.

A lot of times on the job a Christian man especially is subject to ridicule. The enemy will put persons there to ridicule him to try to get him to lose his temper, say words he should not say, or make fun of him because he is faithful to his wife. They say, "Anybody has a right for a little fun. Nobody will know about it." Ridicule! *But the man can't quit the position because he has a family to provide for. So he has to take the ridicule.*

The competition of associates will sometimes depress a man because too much is expected of him. There are demands that he cannot meet or problems for which he cannot find solutions. It is very important that we, as women, understand the pressures that men have.

So what are the two main things that cause pressure on the man? He wants to provide for his family, and he wants to be a success on his job. How can the wife help in this situation?

Proverbs 31:11,12 states:

> **The heart of her husband trusts in her confidently and relies on and believes in her securely, so that he has no lack of [honest] gain or need of [dishonest] spoil.**
> **She comforts, encourages, and does him only good as long as there is life within her.**

---

[8] Proverbs 20:29 TLB - "The glory of young men is their strength; of old men, their experience."

You know that you cannot go to your husband's job and fix things for him. But there are a lot of things that you can do domestically to relieve him of some of the pressures at home. So do these things yourself instead of nagging him to do them. As women we do have the ability to lift the pressure off of our husbands, so let's talk about some of the ways we can do that.

I believe women have the power to break the doom and gloom, bringing their husbands back into good spirits again. In Proverbs 12:4 it says that a woman is a crown to her husband. Proverbs 18:22 talks about how we can make the husband to be a success. I think we must be guided by knowledge of what to do in these situations.

Suggestions

Here are some suggestions:

1. You have the ability to restore self-esteem by giving him compliments. You can call him a winner. If your husband is a builder, you can tell him you know he builds the best houses of all the builders in town; that he is a craftsman, not just a builder. If he is an attorney, you can say, "Honey, any client that you have will be blessed to have you as their attorney." Speak positive to your husband. *You* be the one to encourage him.

If you get into a situation where the husband is not able to provide anymore or is retired, it is really important then because he struggles, realizing he is not able to provide in the same manner in which he did before. Tell him, "Honey, I am so glad that I married you." "Honey, I am so glad that I have the opportunity to spend this time of my life with you." These things are very important to say to a man.

When husbands are retired, they still need those compliments, probably more than ever because they don't get the self-esteem from their co-workers on the job.

2. If a husband comes home depressed and discouraged, you can be gentle and sympathetic toward his situation – the pressure that he

has on his job. This does not mean to join in with his frustration, making statements that will increase his depression and anxiety. Believe for the Holy Spirit to give you words of wisdom, encouragement, and praise.

3. If he comes home after an exceptionally hard day and wants to talk with you about it, don't interrupt him by telling him about your hard day. You may have had one also, but quietly listen to him and encourage him.

> The Holy Spirit will lead you to compliment your husband and build his self-esteem.

I used to say to my husband, "Boy, I wish you could stay here with these four boys and I could go to your job today. Then you would see what I have to do." As I shared earlier, one day I went to his job and worked there for a month. I was glad to get home! I didn't like the pressure that was on the job.

4. When your husband gets home from work, don't tell him the minute he walks in the door the things the children did in not obeying you and expect him to start correcting them before he even says "hello" to them.

5. In the Proverb we are studying today, it says, **"So that he has no lack of [honest] gain or need of [dishonest] spoil"** (Proverbs 31:11). That has to do with finances, and it says he has no lack of honest gain. We need to pray and learn how to reduce expenses. The Holy Spirit will help you do that.

Bill and I have always had to work. It's not like we have always had an abundance of money, but I found I was a pretty good steward and eventually learned to be a better one. You can learn to be a better steward than you are and how to reduce expenses.

Let me tell you a simple thing as I began to come this way and be conscious of this. It is important that as wives we realize that we can make a dollar stretch. When we still had four children at home, the grocery bill was high, but Bill and I have never noticed the inflation of groceries because our grocery bill was such raising four sons that when the groceries went up our family decreased.

I remember praying and asking God to help me with the menus which we will discuss in a later chapter. One day I was in the kitchen and vegetables were the only thing I ever had left over (never any meat). The Holy Spirit said to me, "If you will pour all those vegetables in a bowl and put it in the freezer, the next time you make a stew, you will have your vegetables." That was such a simple thing to do, but I had never done it before. It was because I was conscious of making a dollar stretch and reduce expenses so there would not be any lack.

6. The next thing you can do is reduce the demands on your husband's time. A lot of times when the man walks in the door, you have a hundred honey-do jobs for him to do. Maybe you have been telling him for five weeks that you want these things done, so reduce demands on his time. We must understand the pressure and realize that sometimes they need to sit down in their chair also.

> When there is a lack, sometimes it makes your husband feel like a failure as the provider.

I have to tell you that I have been guilty of doing that. When Bill sat down, I wondered why he wasn't out there raking leaves. Or maybe you just hint a little. One of the things that helped me was to make my husband a honey-do list because one of my *three things* he would like for me to change was that I tried to organize all his free time. He said if he didn't do what I wanted him to do, he felt guilty and if he did what I wanted, then he was upset. That was one of my three things he wanted changed when we started rebuilding our marriage.

Bill wanted me to quit organizing his Saturdays and having all his free time lined up with what I wanted him to do. I prayed about how I could communicate with him without his feeling like I was making demands on his time. So I made him a list of things I would like to have done and I numbered them in priority of what I felt should be done first. I told him I hadn't known that I was bugging him, and I didn't know if he had forgotten them or if he was procrastinating. By making the list, I knew that he would not forget. It got me out of the nagging mode, asking him ten times a day about when he was going to do this or that. After it was on the list, it was up to him, but I did pray.

My best example of this was one Saturday my clothes dryer had something wrong with it. It had been two weeks and still it wasn't fixed. My husband came in the house and said, "Have you been praying about that dryer?" I said, "No, why?" He said, "Well, every time I turn around I hear 'dryer, dryer.'" The Holy Spirit will remind them and let you get off their back. So, if you need something done, just pray about it and you will be surprised how fast it gets done. Reduce the demands on his time.

7. There are some times that we just have to allow for the husband's bad behavior. Sometimes he has had a rough day at work and he comes home grouchy. That is not the time for you to start acting just like he does.

> Two wrongs do not make a right.

What you need to do is have understanding and begin pampering him a little. He needs extra strokes, so allow for his bad behavior. Sometimes he comes home in a foul mood and shows it because he knows you are not going to fire him like possibly could happen on his job. Realize he had pressure at work and give him a quiet time at home. Find something for the children to do after they greet him and give your husband some time to rest.

Now, let me talk about children. If you have children still at home, it is good for the children to greet Daddy, but sometimes Daddy just needs to be quiet. When I began to learn this and work on my marriage, I had something special for them to do so Daddy could have a quiet time. It isn't that they should not greet Daddy or they should not be there, but teach them that Daddy should have his quiet time.

If he goes and sits down in his chair until I get dinner ready, I know that he needs to be quiet or if he comes into the kitchen, that means he is hungry and needs to talk. Sometimes Bill has dinner half eaten by the time I get it on the table. He comes to the stove and samples everything. That used to bug me. I would think, *Well, go ahead and eat out of the pan.* But I am glad he likes my cooking. So it is okay. I don't mind if he wants to come in and sample.

Try to have dinner close to being ready when your husband gets home. If you will get the candle on the table and get the table set, you can be a little late because he will think something is working and going to happen. One day after I got my work done, I put on some beans and made some bean soup and cornbread. When Bill walked in the door, he said, "Oh, it smells so good." Men love that. They love to smell something when they walk through the door. Get your table set early.

> Ladies, our position in the home is like the Church is to Christ. What is the Church doing? Preparing for Christ to come.

Some husbands are home now because they are retired. But for younger women with children, try to make the homecoming of Daddy a happy time. There is nothing wrong with the children taking him to his chair, seating him, and taking his shoes off. He is a special person. It is not just "the old man's home." Take him a cup of coffee or a glass of water. Give him the newspaper. Prop his feet up and give him a kiss. THEN LEAVE HIM ALONE!

After dinner you can get your honey-do stuff. He will be a lot more receptive to do them than if you hit him with the problems when he comes through the door.

You might think, *I can't do that, because I work also and we have a rule that whoever gets home first starts dinner.* This is fine as long as you keep your home a place of refuge and a shelter, a place to get aside from the outside world. But make sure he doesn't come home and have the same pressures that he has on his outside job. (See Proverbs 18:22; Psalm 5:12; and Ephesians 5:25.)

If you do not work outside the home, I recommend that you get to the door and greet him. The lady I traveled with for several years said they had a little poodle which she began to watch. This lady's husband was in and out all day long, and she said, "If he came through that door a hundred times a day, that little dog was at the door wagging his tail." He was meeting him at the door, glad to see him. Let me encourage you to get to the door, be glad to see your husband, and watch the results.

So, the God-given role of the man is lover, leader, protector, and provider. This does not mean that you cannot help in these areas.

Let me give you some scriptures for these roles:

Lover   Ephesians 5:15; Colossians 3:19

Leader   Genesis 3:16; Ephesians 5:23-33

Protector Genesis 2:19; Ephesians 5:29

Provider   Genesis 2:15; 1 Timothy 5:8

Now, let's look at Ephesians 5:23-33:

> For the husband is head of the wife as Christ is Head of the church, Himself the Savior of [His] body.
>
> As the church is subject to Christ, so let wives also be subject in everything to their husbands.
>
> Husbands, love your wives, as Christ loved the church and gave Himself up for her,
>
> So that He might sanctify her, having cleansed her by the washing of water with the Word,
>
> That He might present the church to Himself in glorious splendor, without spot or wrinkle or any such things [that she might be holy and faultless].
>
> Even so husbands should love their wives as [being in a sense] their own bodies. He who loves his own wife loves himself.
>
> For no man ever hated his own flesh, but nourishes and carefully protects and cherishes it, as Christ does the church,
>
> Because we are members (parts) of His body.
>
> For this reason a man shall leave his father and his mother and shall be joined to his wife, and the two shall become one flesh.

This mystery is very great, but I speak concerning [the relation of] Christ and the church.

However, let each man of you [without exception] love his wife as [being in a sense] his very own self; and let the wife see that she respects and reverences her husband [that she notices him, regards him, honors him, prefers him, venerates, and esteems him; and that she defers to him, praises him, and loves and admires him exceedingly].

That is a pretty strong teaching! But this is how we can begin to relieve pressure off of our husband.

A lot of ladies have said to me, "Yes, but it says if he loves her." Listen to what Peter had to say about this:

> Remember, a man wants to fulfill his role, and he wants his wife, more than anyone else in the world, to appreciate his achievements and honor him.

In like manner, you married women, be submissive to your own husbands [subordinate yourselves as being secondary to and dependent on them, and adapt yourselves to them], so that even if any do not obey the Word [of God], they may be won over not by discussion but by the [godly] lives of their wives.

When they observe the pure and modest way in which you conduct yourselves, together with your reverence [for your husband; you are to feel for him all that reverence includes: to respect, defer to, revere him – to honor, esteem, appreciate, prize, and, in the human sense, to adore him, that is, to admire, praise, be devoted to, deeply love, and enjoy your husband].

Let not yours be the [merely] external adorning with [elaborate] interweaving and knotting of the hair, the wearing of jewelry, or changes of clothes;

But let it be the inward adorning and beauty of the hidden person of the heart, with the incorruptible and unfading charm of a gentle and peaceful spirit, which [is not anxious or wrought up, but] is very precious in the sight of God.

For it was thus that the pious women of old who hoped in God were [accustomed] to beautify themselves, and were submissive to their husbands [adapting themselves to them as themselves secondary and dependent upon them].

It was thus that Sarah obeyed Abraham [following his guidance and acknowledging his headship over her by] calling him lord (master, leader, authority). And you are now her true daughters if you do right and let nothing terrify you [not giving way to hysterical fears or letting anxieties unnerve you].

1 Peter 3:1-6

These are the same instructions without requirements for the man.

Mistakes Women Make

Here are some of the mistakes women often make that affect the man's feeling of accomplishment.

Many times a wife will begin to talk about her husband's job like she knows more about it than he does. If he comes home with a problem, the wife will say, "Well, if you would do this and this and this, it would work out better."

Another thing women will do is to show indifference to their husband's achievements. I know a lot of times husbands will want to tell you about a football touchdown they made in high school, how good a player they were when they were eighteen, or how good a golf game they had. Wives will show indifference like, "How many times have I heard that before?" I know I am not the only one who has done this. But when they tell you about their accomplishments, do not treat it with indifference. You need to listen to them.

Another time that women make a mistake and ruin the husband's feeling of accomplishment is trying to excel them in a field where they are trying to win acclaim. If as a couple you work together in the same field, go ahead and treat him as the best in the world, even though you might be just as good as he is.

I will use our marriage as an example. Even though Bill was the Pastor of Cornerstone Church, he and I worked together. If I got in there and tried to get my strokes, my points, my position, trying to win acclaim in the same thing he was doing, it would affect his feeling of accomplishment because he is a man. A wise woman will know how to lift her husband up. Treat him like a king, and you will be treated like a queen.

> You are not to be in competition with your husband. You are to complete him.

A woman's role is equally important but functionally different. It is like a lock and key which make one functioning unit. Both are equally important, but they have different functions.

It is not that their role is more important than yours or that they are better than women. That does not have anything to do with it. What I am trying to say is that women have the ability within them to cause husbands to be lifted up and to function better in their position.

Your husband is to be your primary ministry but not your exclusive ministry. Women can do a lot of things. I do a lot of things, but my primary ministry is to make sure my husband is taken care of. A lot of times there are things I would like to do, but I don't. I get calls for meetings. I gauge how many meetings I do based on what I know my husband wants me to do – as a husband, not as a pastor or minister.

In one situation, when I had completed the meetings for the year, and I know November and December are busy months, I declined an invitation. I told my husband that I had declined an invitation and he said, "I am glad." It is important that we know the things that they would like us to do or not to do.

Your relationship with the Lord is number one, but I am talking about relationships here on earth. YOUR HUSBAND IS TO BE NUMBER ONE!

Another mistake women sometimes make is *asking your husband in a wrong manner.* Many times when you ask your husband to do things at home, you ask in the wrong way. You say, "Do I have to tell you every time to take the trash out?" That is talking down to him like a child. Why not say, "Honey, this is trash day. If you have time, will you please take the trash out?" Most husbands have to be reminded because they are not thinking about domestic duties.

Have you ever been aggravated because you have to ask him? I have. You think, *Why can't he think of it?* Because from their perspective, usually they have something more important to think about. If he forgets, take it out yourself and don't remind him when he comes home that he forgot the trash. It is not worth the division and strife.

Another mistake women sometimes make is *disagreeing with the husband's decisions.* When you disagree with your husband's decision, you should express how you feel, then pray for him and support his right to make the final decision. Remember that God appointed him to be the head of the home. Anything with two heads is a freak. Both cannot be the head, so one will have to make the final decision. Support his right! Do not try to convince him that he is wrong. Do not tell him that he needs to seek counsel, that he'd better go ask his parents. No, you should support his right to make the final decision.

When there are disagreements, pray. Matthew 18:18 KJV says, **"Whatsoever ye shall bind on earth shall be bound in heaven: and whatsoever ye shall loose on earth shall be loosed in heaven."**

Pray like this: *Father, if what my husband is planning to do is not Your will, I bind it in Jesus' name. Do not let it happen. If it is Your will and it happens, then change my heart and my attitude so that we can walk in agreement.*

Amos 3:3 says, **"Do two walk together except they make an appointment and have agreed?"** It is an intentional thing. You are not always going to agree, but I have found when I keep my heart right with the right motive, then God blesses things in our household.

Have you ever disagreed with your husband and later found out that he was right? There might be times when you have disagreed and found out that he was wrong.

Make Your Husband Feel Good as a Provider

Tell your husband that you appreciate his hard work. Do not tell him you will have to seek employment. Do not make comments how you will have to struggle to make his paycheck do. Do not suggest he go for more training in his field so he can earn more.

If you have not told your husband recently how much you appreciate how he has provided for the family, you need to do that. Do not take it for granted that it is his job to make a living.

My dad always worked and provided for our family, so I just figured that was Bill's job. So I never expressed appreciation. But I began to express appreciation out of these teachings.

You need to let your husband know how much you appreciate him – the fact that he gets up, that he goes to work every day, that he is doing his best to provide for his family and retirement. They need appreciation, and it is very important that you speak out about your appreciation.

The Woman's Responsibility in Family Finances

The woman's responsibility in the family finances is making the dollars stretch, and God will help you do that. Learn to shop with the Holy Spirit. If you will take the Holy Spirit with you every place you go, He will help you. And not only that, He will help you plant in other people's lives and then your household will be blessed.

Necessities

I have a reason for saying that. Sometimes in our economy, there is a real need for just the necessities, but most of us have more than that. There has been an attitude in the past that the man is responsible to provide luxuries. *He does not have the responsibility for that.*

> A man is responsible to provide the necessities – shelter, food, and a minimal amount of clothing.

Women have needs, wants, and desires in life. But women need to learn to be content with what they have. A woman should not want her husband to work three jobs so she can drive a newer car or have a new couch. That should not be the goal. Women should recognize the competition in the world and in the television advertisements that would create a dissatisfied spirit in them if they are not on their guard.

I have dealt with women where the shopping channel has created a real disaster in their lives. It can cause you to want and want and want, tempting you and tempting you until it really becomes a disaster. God calls it lust.[9]

I went to a lady's home who was really hooked on television advertising. Her bed was piled high with stuff that she had never used. That was her entertainment. She was at home in the daytime watching the shopping channel and buying stuff. I can tell you, it can be a disaster. I am not saying, "Do not watch it," but I am saying, "Do not get hooked on it." I think it is as bad as the soaps because it really is a temptation. I don't want to put you under condemnation, but it is a real problem that I find in some women's lives today.

Spending does not bring happiness. We are a three-part person. We have a soul (our mind, will, and emotions), we have a spirit, and we live in a body. Our mind and emotions (we call it our "flesh") are

---

[9] 1 John 2:16,17 KJV - "**For all that is in the world, the lust of the flesh, and the lust of the eyes, and the pride of life, is not of the Father, but is of the world. And the world passeth away, and the lust thereof: but he that doeth the will of God abideth for ever.**"

never content. You get one new thing and you want another new thing. Flesh always wants more.

"Things" will never fill the hole in your soul. When you see a person who is impulsively buying and always shopping, this person has a hole in their soul that they are trying to fill with things, but it will not happen. It has to be filled with your relationship with Jesus Christ. You can feel like you are a queen and not wear a $500 dress. Fulfillment only comes from your relationship with Jesus Christ.

Do you ever say the following? "I wish we had more money. The Jones' got a new car, furniture, house, etc." If you envy people who live in larger houses than you do, drive better cars, have better clothing, what you need to do sometime is drive through the part of town where they don't have what you have, and you will be happy to go home. Having an attitude of gratitude will bring contentment which equals peace. (Philippians 4:11.)

Do you complain that there is not enough money to go around or suggest your husband take a part-time job to provide luxuries? If you are always complaining about what you don't have, *it will make your husband feel like a failure as a provider.*

Should a Wife Have a Budget?

Yes, you should have a budget, and your household should have a budget. I like to budget my own life and have some guidelines to live with. At the time I made a budget for myself, we still had children at home and I was not working. Bill always deposited all of his check, but there was a certain amount I got for grocery money and a little bit of spending money. When Bill and I began to work on our finances, he asked me how much I needed a week to run the house. I started to say a million dollars, but I didn't! I told him based on what I thought it was.

Through the financial classes which I attended, we were instructed to keep a list of everything we spent. In about two weeks' time, I had to go back to him and say, "Honey, I didn't tell you enough because I forgot about the children's lunch money." I showed him my list, and he said, "You know what? You are right." So he allowed me more money for household expenses.

There was another thing it did. Because I was being a good steward of the money I had, I was using my coupons for grocery shopping and saving the balance of money in a sugar bowl. Bill felt like I should not be spending the money I had saved in the sugar bowl. I said, "Well, Honey, I have been a good steward, cutting coupons and reading the ads." He said, "You know, you are right." I got to keep the money in the sugar bowl so it was another incentive for me to be a good steward.

Since I was not working outside the home, I didn't have any "income," but we never felt like the money was his and hers; it was ours. Just because a woman does not work outside the home, whatever the husband brings in is hers also. If men had to pay for what a wife does in the home, most, if not all, could not afford it.

Whatever our income is, it is ours and we manage it together. I would make a list of every bill that had to be paid each month. My bookkeeping system was not fancy. I had a tablet and I listed tithes first, house next, utilities, and insurance. It was listed on a monthly basis so when we got paid on the first and fifteenth, Bill and I would sit down, go over the list, and pay the things that needed to be paid so they were on time and we marked those things paid. I wrote all of the checks, or 95 percent of them, but Bill knew what was going on.

When we started getting our relationship together, he had no idea of what anything cost. He just deposited his check. I remember when I took him to the store the first time to buy jeans for the boys, he thought they were still $3.98. Then, I remember the first time I brought a new outfit home, and hung it on the door with the price tag still on it. Bill looked at the jacket and said, "Is that for all four pieces, a weekender?" I said, "No, Honey, that is for the jacket." So another thing I did was to get honest with him about how much things cost. I had always hated to tell him because he thought I spent too much money and he would be concerned about the finances.

It is important to get honest in your finances. Remember, Proverbs 31 says, **"He has no lack of [honest] gain or need of [dishonest] spoil"** (v. 11).

Should a wife have a budget? Yes. If so, what should it include? You decide. Should she be able to keep the money saved from the budget? Yes.

If you handle the finances in your home, is it because you want to or is it a necessity? I realize that some women are better stewards of money than men are. Some men have problems with finances too. I am not saying who should handle the finances, but I think everyone should be informed.

The other thing is, many times the person who manages the finances is in control. You want to make sure you are not managing the finances because you want control. Check your heart motive as to why you are managing the finances, if you are. Also, I don't think women should be ignorant about finances. They should know what is going on. They should know about insurance and bank accounts.

If your husband is not allowing you to be a part of the finances, you need to pray for him. Also, sometimes out of experiences, men do not think they can trust women in finances. So you may be paying the price especially if you are in a second marriage because of what someone else has done. You need to give him time to learn to trust you. When he sees that he can trust you, then he will be more open and share things with you.

Impulsive Buying

Here are eight things concerning impulsive buying that helped me in my life. I had a problem with impulsive buying. I am sure I was trying to fill a hole in my soul, but also one of my personality traits is being impulsive. I had an attitude that if there were still checks in the checkbook, there was still money in the bank. *Impulsive buying will ruin the budget.*

1. Use cash. I learned to use cash. I don't use cash all the time today because I have corrected my problem. Some of you need plastic surgery (cut up credit cards). My husband gave me plastic surgery. It is okay to have credit cards if you can control your cards and not let them control you. That is the key.

2. When you go shopping, take only as much money as you plan to spend.

3. Don't take people with you who encourage you to buy something you do not want or need.

4. If in doubt, don't buy. Pray about what you buy. Always let the peace of God rule in your heart. I want to tell you that every time I have gone against that peace, I hated what I bought. The sales person will try to sell you, telling you how good it looks, that you need it and that you deserve it. All they are doing is working on their commission check. I know because I used to sell clothes. I wasn't dishonest with people, because I really enjoyed helping ladies look good. But I am just encouraging you to stay in control.

5. If an item is more than $20, unless you planned it, do not buy at that time but go home and think about it overnight. We are talking about impulsive buying. If it is yours, it will still be there. A lot of times I would go home, think about it, and decide that I didn't need it or I didn't want it. I could use that $20 someplace else.

6. Don't buy anything, no matter how great it is or how terrific the bargain is, if you can't afford it or if you need something else more.

7. This is hard on me because I love sales, but beware of sales as they encourage impulsive buying. I believe in sales if you have enough control and let the Holy Spirit guide you.

8. When doing extensive shopping like fall clothing, Christmas, furniture, etc., make a preliminary shopping trip. Go to several stores and ask questions. The next day or the next week you will be better able to evaluate what you have seen. It will take time, but it will save money.

Christmas Shopping

I had the privilege of raising four children and in Christmas shopping, it was important to make our dollars stretch. Here are my suggestions for your Christmas shopping:

1. Get a Christmas catalog, such as Sears or J. C. Penney's.

2. Have the children look through the catalog and put their initial on things they would like to have. This is great entertainment.

3. Have them look back through the catalog and number by desire (1, 2, 3) the things they would like.

4. Make a list of their desires.

5. Take the list and make a preliminary trip to check prices and availability.

6. Make a second trip to make purchases. *Only buy the items on the list.* Stores are always loaded with cute items at Christmas. This creates an atmosphere for impulsive buying.

7. If you are buying for grandchildren, it is not okay to be impulsive and blow the budget. I have to be careful with my grandchildren because stores have so many cute little things, and those things can really mount up in our spending.

Updating Wardrobe

Proverbs 31:22 says, **"She makes for herself coverlets, cushions, and rugs of tapestry. Her clothing is of linen, pure and fine, and of purple [such as that of which the clothing of the priests and the hallowed cloths of the temple were made]."**

Be clean and care how you look and smell, both at home and outside of the home. Appearance commands respect.

In updating my wardrobe and purchasing clothes, first I go to different stores when the season gets ready to change and look to see what colors they are putting together. Then I go back to my closet and begin to put colors together that will be in style for the season. I get a couple of catalogs, look through them, and say, "Hey, I can take my black dress and do something like that," or, "I can take that jacket and make that happen." If you do that, you will build a better wardrobe than if you just go and buy what is in style.

Always do your major buying in basic things that you can redo and recycle. If you keep your clothes basic, you can make a very small investment in things that will update it. Learn to shop at home in your closet.

Always buy things that are fads or accessories in small amounts like a scarf or earrings. If it is an animal print like leopard (I love leopard), I don't have to buy a lot because I have saved leopard accessories (scarf, blouse, and earrings) that are ten to fifteen years old. Usually, I keep these items season after season.

Here is my suggestion for major buying. Buy two suits, for example black and red, and buy another skirt and slacks that will mix with both jackets. Buy five tops (sweaters and blouses). Then, by mixing and matching, you will have thirty-five outfits.

The Eighty-Two-Year-Old Salesman

The eighty-two-year-old salesman was getting an award for being the best natured businessman of the year. He credited his wife for his happy nature, his good spirits, and his good temper. He said, "Without her I might have had many ulcers, many heart attacks, or nervous depressions during my sixty-five years of sales."

He told the doctors who had made the award to the impressed businessmen the importance of cutting down on stress and strain. "Every morning when I get up, I hear my wife singing as she prepares breakfast." (I don't think any man should walk out of the door with his wife in bed. You can go back to bed if you need a nap later, but you need to send your husband off to work. Make sure he gets his first kiss and compliment of the day from you and not from someone else.)

This salesman explained, "When I come to the table, she straightens my tie, gives me a big kiss, and tells me how handsome I am, and I am eighty-two. She also tells me that she is proud I am such a wonderful fellow and that all her women friends are jealous. Then she feeds me, puts a flower in my lapel, and sends me off to work. I feel so good I find myself treating everybody the way she treats me," said the bald little man with his Charlie Chaplin mustache. "When I come home at night, my wife gives me the same happy treatment. I don't know why all wives don't behave that way," he concluded.

Prayer

Father, we thank You for our lesson today. We pray that You will help us to be doers of Your Word and not hearers only. It doesn't make any difference how many years we have been married, there is always room for improvement. I thank You that every woman who reads this book — married or single — will receive this teaching and take it and teach it to other women and counsel and help them.

God, help each one with their relationship with other people. Father, I pray for every married woman reading this that You would give her an attitude of respect and reverence toward her husband, that she realize that this is the ministry You have called her to, and let her see that her ministry to her husband is important.

> Wives, you have a lot more to do with your husbands' success than you realize.

Thank You, Father, for the men You have given these readers. You said it was not good for man to be alone. Let the wives have the attitude that he is a special gift from You. May the wives understand the pressures of their husbands. Father, thank You that the husbands whose wives are reading this book will be reminded that everything they put their hands to will prosper. I pray that wives will begin to pray for them and see their husbands elevated and lifted up.

We bind mistakes and wasted time. God, we thank You that both the wives and the husbands have favor, that they walk blessed in their homes, and that they will be a blessing to everyone who is there.

We ask these things in Jesus' precious name. Amen.

Nuggets from Chapter 4

In this chapter, we talked about understanding the pressures of the man. Man's first pressure is from God. His second pressure is financial. His third pressure is position and status in the workplace and in the family.

A wife can be a helpmeet to her husband by:

1. Complimenting him.
2. Being sympathetic.
3. Quietly listening to him and encouraging him.
4. Not giving him problems the minute he walks through the door.
5. Learning how to reduce expenses.
6. Not making demands on his time.
7. Allowing him to be disagreeable sometimes.
8. Leaving him alone when he is tired.
9. Not being in competition with him but completing him.
10. Asking your husband in a correct manner.
11. Learning to handle cash and avoid impulsive buying.

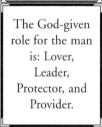

The God-given role for the man is: Lover, Leader, Protector, and Provider.

CHAPTER
5

Inner and Outer Beauty of the Woman

As a review, are you working on writing the twenty good things about yourself? Have you written the ten good things about your husband? Have you placed the "look" signs around your house? Did your husband give you his list of the three things he wanted you to change? Did you share the ten good things about your husband with him? If you did, he is probably on Cloud 9 right now!

Let me share a testimony of a lady who did this assignment. She and her husband were separated, but she made the list of ten good things and gave it to him when he came to see the children. He didn't say anything. Sometimes men do not know how to handle these things. But three months later, they were at a convention in New York and they were back together again.

When he emptied his pockets and put things on the dresser, there was this little crumpled paper in his pocket. It was the list she had given him which he was carrying in his pocket. He was a professional man, very successful, yet he carried his wife's list in his pocket.

A lot of times we take men for granted, never giving them anything except criticism, or we try to straighten them up like we think they should be. Really, words go a long way. After we get married, we begin to see all the negatives, all the weaknesses, and major on them. Then couples begin to drift apart.

> Never underestimate the power of words. Men really want your approval.

Some husbands might be fearful of giving you the list of three things. I know Bill was fearful of doing that, and when he came home for dinner the night before my next class, I said, "Honey, I really am trying to be a better wife, and I need your list." He just looked at me.

As he started out the door, he came back and I was still sitting at the dinner table. He said, "Oh, by the way, here is your list." He pitched it on the table and went out the door quickly. I still remember those things today, and sometimes I still have to work on them.

Be sure to put up your "look" signs, even if you are single, because it will remind you to look to the good of any situation and look for the good in other people. It will help you in your attitude.

I want to give you our scripture again from which we took the title for this book:

> **But thanks be to God, Who in Christ always leads us in triumph [as trophies of Christ's victory] and through us spreads and makes evident the fragrance of the knowledge of God everywhere.**
> **For we are the sweet fragrance of Christ [which exhales] unto God, [discernible alike] among those who are being saved and among those who are perishing.**
>
> 2 Corinthians 2:14,15

My goal is to have every woman know so much and be so confident of who she is in Christ Jesus that she can minister, not only in her home but outside the home. And whatever circumstance she is in, she becomes that sweet-smelling fragrance. Too many times a woman's fragrance is not good in a situation, and she does not leave that sweet-smelling fragrance when she departs.

100

I often think of husbands when they leave home and the last words they hear are wives criticizing them, when they should be leaving with the feeling that the person they left behind the closed door is the person to whom they want to return.

What would be their last picture of you in the home, not only your mouth but your appearance? It doesn't take you long to run a brush through your hair, use a little mouthwash, and put on a little lipstick so you smell good when they leave.

A lot of times women try to preach to their family before they go to school or work each morning, and their breath smells so bad the family can't get near enough to hear them.

When your husband left this morning, did he leave behind that closed door a person and an atmosphere of a sweet-smelling fragrance that he wants to come back to in the evening? Did your family leave with that kind of atmosphere in the home?

It is so important that we become a sweet-smelling fragrance where we go or whatever we do. So in this chapter, I want to talk to you about the inner beauty of a woman. The world might call her a model woman, a number ten. And I want to let you know that you are a number ten in the Kingdom of God if you are a Christian. God has nothing but beautiful daughters.

> We should be a sweet-smelling fragrance in every area of our life – spirit, soul, and body.

It is important that we talk about this portion of your life. I think it is important that you realize (and we taught this in chapter 2) who you are in Christ Jesus, but also that you know you are the temple of the Holy Spirit who dwells in you. Proverbs 31 gives much instruction as to how the temple was to be taken care of. And since we are the temple, I think God cares about how His daughters are clothed – inner beauty and outer beauty.

Let's look at Proverbs 31:13-22 again:

She seeks out wool and flax and works with willing hands [to develop it].

She is like the merchant ships loaded with foodstuffs; she brings her household's food from a far [country].

She rises while it is yet night and gets [spiritual] food for her household and assigns her maids their tasks.

She considers a [new] field before she buys or accepts it [expanding prudently and not courting neglect of her present duties by assuming other duties]; with her savings [of time and strength] she plants fruitful vines in her vineyard.

She girls herself with strength [spiritual, mental, and physical fitness for her God-given task] and makes her arms strong and firm.

She tastes and sees that her gain from work [with and for God] is good; her lamp goes not out, but it burns on continually through the night [of trouble, privation, or sorrow, warning away fear, doubt, and distrust].

She lays her hands to the spindle, and her hands hold the distaff.

She opens her hand to the poor, yes, she reaches out her filled hands to the needy [whether in body, mind, or spirit].

She fears not the snow for her family, for all her household are doubly clothed in scarlet.

She makes for herself coverlets, cushions, and rugs of tapestry. Her clothing is of linen, pure and fine, and of purple [such as that of which the clothing of the priests and the hallowed cloths of the temple were made].

Verse 13 says she seeks out the wool and flax and works with willing hands to develop it. In those days the women had to make the material that they made their garments out of.

One day I was sitting on the couch meditating on this portion of Scripture, as I think every portion of the Bible is important. It is not "generational" – meaning it's not like it was just for people long ago and not for us today. I believe there is a spiritual or a practical meaning in the Word for every area of your life.

So I said, "Lord, tell me about the wool and flax." I do good to get a button sewed on, and I could not see how it applied to me. I heard, "Well, what is wool?" I thought of the white stuff – the wool – sheared off of lambs. I heard the Holy Spirit say, "What do you use wool for?" I said, "Well, blankets, coats, and covering." Then I heard, "She seeks out the covering for her household, working with willing hands to develop it."

I believe you should seek out the Word of God for a covering for your household – a covering of God's Word and prayer, the protection of God's Word, and work with willing hands to develop it. It doesn't just happen overnight. You have to develop a covering for your household, continuing to learn the Word of God and applying it as a covering.

When your family is gone in the daytime, you can have the Christian radio or TV music on. Don't have the soap operas or negative talk shows on because your life is never going to turn that way. Thank God! A lot of times you can let come through on your radio or television what you would not let come through the front door. Don't allow ungodly things to fill your household, but have positive and good things filling your house. So it is very important that you cover and protect your household.

Now, you could get some practical meaning out of that and say she makes things, her bed coverings, and things like that, but this is what the Holy Spirit told me for my life. He said that I could continually develop the spiritual covering for my household. I do that even today. Our children are gone. They do not live with us, but I continue daily to cover them with the Word of God and prayer and make sure they are protected.

> An ideal woman will see to it that her household is covered with the Word of God

Our son, Tom, traveled to Italy and Europe twice in one month. He was to come home on a Thursday or Friday. All that day I kept covering him with the blood of Jesus. He was continually on my heart. I could reason and say it was because I had made that trip and knew it was a long way home. I just kept covering him with the blood of Jesus.

We went to the airport with his wife and two children to meet him on Friday evening. He looked very worn out because he had had a very difficult time getting home. He had turned his rental car in, left the hotel, and when he got to the airport in Italy, they had no reservation for him and no more planes going out. He had ridden buses, he had ridden everything just to get back to the states that night. I believe the blood of Jesus kept covering him and kept directing him, and even though he was physically tired, he arrived home safely.

Sometimes when you are in these situations, there are principalities, powers, and rulers of darkness that would like to destroy. I believe that we have the responsibility as women to keep our house covered and keep our household protected.

Proverbs 31 says she brings her household's food from a far country. I shared on that in a previous chapter. I believe it has two applications. You have the ability to be good stewards, to shop and bring your household food from those good bargains. But from a spiritual standpoint, it is good to go to a women's conference or a Bible study and take your household spiritual food from a far country. It is important that you keep yourselves refreshed so that you are bringing fresh food, fresh manna from heaven. It will help you set the atmosphere in your home. Even if you have a godly husband, you will set the godly atmosphere in your home.

In a Christian family class we were teaching, Jim, our third son, shared that when he recommitted his life to the Lord, every time he opened his mouth, a scripture would come out. He thought, *I have never read the Bible all the way through.* He wondered, *Where did I get all this scripture? What is it?* Then he realized (and no glory to me) that I had spoken the Word of God to him as a child and as a teenager. And when he came back to the Lord, he did not learn all that, even though he has diligently studied the Word of God. It was placed in his spirit by the scriptures I had spoken. He has spoken to the young people at Cornerstone Church regarding the importance of studying the Word of God.

So it is important that you bring that spiritual food from a far country. I appreciate ladies who come from other churches to Ladies' Bible Study because they are taking back spiritual food for their household and also to the people in their churches. You can take that spiritual food and set other people free with the Word of God.

> She rises while it is yet night and gets [spiritual] food for her household and assigns her maids their tasks. She considers a [new] field before she buys or accepts it [expanding prudently and not courting neglect of her present duties by assuming other duties]. . . .

Proverbs 31:15,16

In verse 19, it says, **"She lays her hands to the spindle, and her hands hold the distaff."** As I began to study that, I realized that as she lays her hand to the spindle, it is like a spinning wheel. There is one hand that is holding things in balance and the other hand is guiding. That is just like a mother. A mother is always balancing the household. She is a peacemaker. She brings peace among the children. She is the one listening to the Spirit of God. Not only is she holding things in balance, she is also guiding while she is doing that.

My mother taught me that busy hands are happy hands. It is the hands that lay idle that bring discontent and depression. I have never seen a person in depression who is busy, unless that person has some kind of chemical imbalance. A person who is busy does not have depression, because he or she doesn't have time. Depression does not have time to catch up with him or her.

All of us have the opportunity to be depressed. But you get up, you get out of it, and the evil one cannot attach himself to you unless there is a chemistry imbalance. Remember, there are two things that we are talking about: emotion and chemistry. But I have never seen a depressed person who was busy guiding, balancing, and doing those things. Keeping busy is a good cure for depression.

Verses 20 and 21 say, **"She opens her hand to the poor, yes, she reaches out her filled hands to the needy [whether in body, mind, or**

105

spirit]. **She fears not the snow for her family, for all her household are doubly clothed in scarlet.**" What is scarlet? It is the precious blood of Jesus. She does not wait for the Sunday school teacher or someone at her church to lead her child to Jesus. She makes sure her child knows Jesus.

Many a person has been saved right at their table with cookies and milk when they came home from school. Let me share this with you. One of the things I learned in raising four children is that children have been under pressure all day at school. When they walk through the door, they do not need Mama to start giving them orders. Just have some cookies and milk on the table. It is much easier to win a little child to the Lord with a tummy full of cookies and milk and a good atmosphere.

A few years ago, I had the opportunity to stay with two of my grandchildren while their parents went out of town. I got to be with them for a week. I was standing at the door when they got off the bus in the afternoon. As they stepped through the door, I didn't say, "Get your homework done, etc." I had a snack or something for them to do – a treat for them when they got home. They had thirty minutes to unwind.

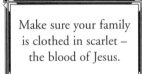

Make sure your family is clothed in scarlet – the blood of Jesus.

Children are just like you are. You do not like to come through the door and see the dirty dishes and a dirty house. They need some time to relax and then they will be ready to do their homework and get their chores done. Do not let them come through the door and get a continual flow of what they have had at school all day.

So I believe you have the ability to reach out your hands to the needy and cover your household with the precious blood of Jesus.

Virtues You Need in Your Life

We all need to check to see if we have these virtues in our lives.

Second Peter 1:1,2 states:

> Simon Peter, a servant and apostle (special messenger) of Jesus Christ, to those who have received (obtained an equal privilege of) like precious faith with ourselves in and through the righteousness of our God and Savior Jesus Christ:
> May grace (God's favor) and peace (which is perfect well-being, all necessary good, all spiritual prosperity, and freedom from fears and agitating passions and moral conflicts) be multiplied to you in [the full, personal, precise, and correct] knowledge of God and of Jesus our Lord.

I want you to notice the greeting that Simon Peter gives to people. He does not immediately begin to give them instruction. What is his greeting? He says, "May grace be to you, peace be to you, may you be prosperous." The way you greet people and the way you treat your family are so important.

I have to tell you that a lot of times I have to work on this, because after quite a few telephone calls, there are a lot of things I am concerned about. So when Pastor walks in the door, I say, "I need to talk to you about this, this, and this," I forget that he needs to get in his chair for a little while. He never fusses at me, but all of a sudden it is like he has already got a whole day, ten hours, on his shoulders. He walks through the front door and I put more on him. Yes, I need to talk to him, but I can wait. It is not such a crisis that it has to be handled immediately.

Notice what Peter did. He didn't just blurt out all the problems and give you all the instructions. He begins to talk to you about having grace and peace and being prosperous. You will notice that his greeting is one that makes you want to hear his instructions. A lot of times your greetings keep your instructions from being heard or what you wanted to share because you already blew the whole thing with the first words out of your mouth.

Second Peter 1:3-7 says:

For His divine power has bestowed upon us all things that [are requisite and suited] to life and godliness, through the [full, personal] knowledge of Him Who called us by and to His own glory and excellence (virtue).

By means of these He has bestowed on us His precious and exceedingly great promises, so that through them you may escape [by flight] from the moral decay (rottenness and corruption) that is in the world because of covetousness (lust and greed), and become sharers (partakers) of the divine nature.

For this very reason, adding your diligence [to the divine promises], employ every effort in exercising your faith to develop virtue (excellence, resolution, Christian energy), and in [exercising] virtue [develop] knowledge (intelligence).

And in [exercising] knowledge [develop] self-control, and in [exercising] self-control [develop] steadfastness (patience, endurance), and in [exercising] steadfastness [develop] godliness (piety).

And in [exercising] godliness [develop] brotherly affection and in [exercising] brother affection [develop] Christian love.

In verse 5, Peter starts listing those virtues:

1. *Diligence.* To what? To the divine promises. How much diligence do you have in your life? Are you diligent to study the Word of God? Are you diligent to do the things you know to do? Are you diligent to pray? Are you diligent to take care of your family and to keep your home? Are you a diligent person in your habits? For twenty-one days if you read a chapter of the Bible, you will find that you will begin to be a diligent person. You need to read those things over and over for twenty-one days. Be diligent to pay your bills on time. Be diligent to attend church. Do everything to be diligent to the divine promises.

2. *Faith.* Employ every effort in exercising your faith. The Word tells us that every person has been given a measure of faith. You have faith or you would not be in the Kingdom of God. You would not have accepted Jesus as your personal Lord and Savior.

Have you exercised your faith? Some people have more faith than others because they have exercised it. They watered that little seed of faith with the Word of God. As you exercise it, as you water it with the water of the Word, your faith will begin to grow.

Some people say, "I don't have anything to give." I heard the story of a man telling about giving when he was first converted. He said he was at one meeting and he did not have anything to give when they passed the offering plate. But he had received a visitor's card and a pen with the church's name on it. Since he had nothing to give, he put the pen back in the offering plate as an act of faith. He exercised his faith. Before he left, someone handed him $20 so he ran back to find the offering plate and gave that $20. I do not care if it is just a penny, begin to put some seed in the offering or do something to develop your faith.

It is hard to believe for your healing when you really get attacked with something like cancer if you can't believe for the healing of a headache. It is hard to believe for cake when you have never believed for a slice of bread. You might say, "But I pray sometimes and things don't happen." If that is your situation, keep exercising your faith. It is your part to keep believing. It is God's part to do the blessing.

Sometimes we give up just before the blessing comes in. Not only that, but we negate what we prayed by what we speak out of our mouth after praying. Someone may ask you how you are doing. You reply, "Well, under the circumstances. . . ." What are you doing under the circumstances when you are supposed to be on top? You are the head and not the tail. You are above and not beneath. So it is important what you say after you pray. Learn to exercise your faith.

3. *Virtue* means excellence, resolution, Christian energy. Webster defines "virtue" as conformity to a standard of right, moral excellence, and a commendable quality or trait.[10]

4. *Knowledge and Understanding.* The reason for this teaching is that you will have knowledge and understanding of the Word of God. I shared earlier that I had read the Bible through two or three times. I

read it like a history book – not like a "how-to" book. But when I began to find in the Bible instructions about marriage and family, I started studying the Bible. The only thing I had heard previously was on Mother's Day and the minister would say, "Wives, obey your husbands." I thought, *Me obey him? You have got to be kidding!* I am still learning and I have been born again since I was nine years of age. You will never get through learning. When you get through learning, you are through.

Do not think you know it all. That is why we have classes so you can learn about people and you can learn about marriage. Another thing, don't get set in your ways. I know when you get older, you think you have the picture just right. I tell you about the time I think I have got it right, something will blow me away, and I have to learn all over again. So I am saying to you, you have to have that knowledge and understanding.

Proverbs 24:3,4 says a home is built through wisdom, understanding, and knowledge. Three key things: wisdom, understanding, and knowledge.

5. *Self-control or Temperance.* You can only have self-control through the Spirit of God on the inside of you, growing and renewing your mind. But if you do not feed your spirit man on the Word of God, then your flesh is going to control you, and flesh is never content. Flesh will want one more thing. Flesh will want to get the last word in. That is what causes the drug and alcohol addictions. The flesh starts out with a little, but always wants more and more. Impulsive buying, for example, is a spirit. So you have to have self-control or temperance in your life.

6. *Patience, Steadfastness, Endurance.* I love how the Word says it: "Develop steadfastness (patience/endurance)." Do not pray for patience. You already have the fruit in your life. You just have to exer-

---

[10] *Webster's New Collegiate Dictionary* (Springfield, MA: A Merriam-Webster, G & C Merriam Co., 1977), p. 1100.

cise it. I had a little sign on the wall of my home in Tulsa that said, "Please be patient with me. God is not finished with me yet."

We need to be patient with other people. God is not through with them yet either. Allow for the imperfections. Allow for their weaknesses and be patient with them. Then you will have that stead-fastness so that people will know you are not going to get upset with them. Be patient in all situations.

> The stronger your spirit, the weaker your flesh.

Hebrews 6:12 KJV says, **"That ye be not slothful, but followers of them who through faith and patience inherit the promises."** This is a two-fold requirement: It is not enough to have faith, you must also have patience. After you ask, how soon do you want God's answer? Some will answer, "Last night." They do not want to wait until God answers. Sometimes He is working out things in your life.

Also, sometimes you can get impatient, wanting your husband to do things sooner than he is doing them. You might say, "Come on, let's get on with this thing. If you would just come on, we could accomplish these things for the Kingdom of God." No, through *faith* and *patience* you inherit the promises.

In our relationship, I have been the extrovert, my husband the introvert. You know, I thank God for him. He has kept me from burning out. When I was ninety miles down the road from him, saying, "Come on, come on, come on," he was saying, "No, let's wait." But then he sped up a little and I slowed down. Now we are walking together.

7. *Godliness.* Galatians 5:22 says if you are filled with the Spirit of God, you have that self-control and you have that temperance in your life. You have the fruit, but you have to water it so it will grow. "Godliness" just means that you have a godly attitude.

Romans 12:1,2 KJV says:

> I beseech you therefore, brethren, by the mercies of God, that ye present your bodies a living sacrifice, holy, acceptable unto God, which is your reasonable service.
>
> And be not conformed to this world: but be ye transformed by the renewing of your mind, that ye may prove what is that good, and acceptable, and perfect, will of God.

Do not be conformed to this world, but be transformed by the renewing of your mind. The world is talking a lot about the election, among other things. You have heard all the negative things, but you need to have a godly attitude toward the election. Whoever our president is, you need to begin to pray for him and respect him, regardless of what party he belongs to. God's Word says to honor those who have the rule over you. Whether you like it or not, you need to have a godly attitude, so develop godliness in your life.

8. *Love and Kindness.* This means godly love, which is *agape* love. This is the First Corinthians 13:4-8 kind of love. Love hardly notices when something is done wrong. Do not keep score. Develop the godly love. It does not seek its own way or its own rights.

I will tell you what I did with First Corinthians 13:4-8, which helped me develop godliness in my life. I took that chapter and I put my name in it: "Janet hardly notices when she has been done wrong. She always looks for the best in the other person. She is not self-seeking. She doesn't seek her own ways or her own rights." I wrote it out and put it on my mirror so I could look at it every morning when I started doing these lessons.

Write your name in these verses, and read it out loud daily. It will change your actions. The Holy Spirit will convict you.

9. *Appearance, Domestic Qualities, and Honesty or Trustworthiness.* Hebrews 6:12 KJV says, **"That ye be not slothful, but followers of *them who through faith and patience inherit the promises.*"**

Second Peter 1:8,9 says:

For as these qualities are yours and increasingly abound in you, they will keep [you] from being idle or unfruitful unto the [full personal] knowledge of our Lord Jesus Christ (the Messiah, the Anointed One).

For whoever lacks these qualities is blind, [spiritually] shortsighted, seeing only what is near to him, and has become oblivious [to the fact] that he was cleansed from his old sins.

Examine Yourself

Now I want to ask you some questions. I want you to grade yourself on these before the next chapter. No one is going to see your test grades. Take your points from one to five with five being the highest. See what areas you need to improve. That is a goal we are all reaching for. I am still pressing toward that mark. How did you grade yourself?

1. *Are you a happy person, very happy, frequently unhappy, or unhappy most of the time?*

As I looked in my life some twenty-six years ago, I was really in drudgery. Here I was a personality that laughed at parties or whatever, but when I got into marriage and raising the children, I got so down in a rut. I remember going to dinner with my family. I don't know why they even sat at the same table with me because I was so long-faced. I mean, who would have wanted to be around me? The Holy Spirit began to tell me that. He talked to me about my face. You know a lot of things we wear in our life do not cost money, and our facial expression is one of them.

There is an old saying, "Smile and the world smiles with you; cry and you cry alone." I began to realize that I was not a happy person. I really didn't have that much to be unhappy about. I do not say the circumstances were all okay. I didn't have a perfect set of circumstances, but there was not anything so bad that I had to be unhappy

> It doesn't cost a penny to smile, and you will feel better.

and long-faced all the time. Nobody wants to come home to an old long face. So what did I do?

I did something very spiritual. I began to read comics again, and I looked for jokes in magazines and things like that. And I began to laugh at whatever I could – the way the cat played. I began to make myself laugh again so I wouldn't be a long-faced person that people would not want to talk with. When you smile and you are a happy person to be around, you will have more friends than you know what to do with.

One of the reasons people are lonely is because they are long-faced and negative and no one wants to be around them. I know it is hard for you to believe that I had to learn to smile again, but I did and you can too.

I realize that if you are a melancholy person, you need to be taught to smile because you were born a serious baby, but you can smile.

2. *Have you made Jesus the Lord of your life?* I want to give you some scriptures to read on this: Romans 3:23; John 3:16; 1 John 1:9; and Romans 10:9-13. Life is more than just attending church and having salvation. If you confess with your mouth and believe in your heart that Jesus died for your sins, you are saved. Make Jesus the Lord of your life.

Jesus became my Savior when I was nine years of age, but Jesus became my Lord at age forty. That means you get off the throne of your life and put Him on the throne. You do what His Word says to do whether you feel like it or not. I do not get a hundred on that, but Jesus is my Lord today. *He was my Savior, but now He is my Lord and Savior.* That means He is boss. So it is important to ask yourself this question: Is Jesus your Lord?

At forty years of age and out of a desperate situation, I knelt at a chair and said, "God, I have got to have You in my life if it means I have to do this, this, and this," which had to do with obedience, some things my husband wanted me to do. I said, "I have got to have You," and Jesus became my Lord.

Later on, I shared with my husband what happened. I know I was a Christian, but it was just like I got saved. I had just been born again. Little did I know that night Jesus became my Lord the wonderful plans God had for me.

Matthew 6:33 KJV says, **"Seek ye first the kingdom of God, and his righteousness; and all these things shall be added unto you."** Is Jesus your Lord?

3. *Do you read your Bible daily?* If not, is it because you don't know where to start? You have too busy a schedule? You read but you do not understand and find it boring?

I knew how to read cover to cover, but I did not know how to study the Word of God. My schedule was very busy. I had four children. I would read, but I didn't understand, so I got some self-help books, and I want to recommend that to you.

The first thing I took was *God's Creative Power* by Charles Capps. I underlined all those scriptures in my Bible. If you don't have a Bible that you can underline in, get one. I underlined these scriptures so when I went through my Bible, I knew those applied to me. Not only that, I would read just a chapter a day. I learned to ask myself, "What does this mean to me?" It was as if I got a letter in the mail, "What does this say to me?"

I would read Psalms. There is just one chapter in Proverbs for each day of the month, so read a chapter in Proverbs each day.

If you have not read a Bible before, I would recommend that you read the New Testament. It is a good place to start, and ask yourself, "What does it mean to me?" Then I would say, "Did I find anything in there that would change my situation or circumstance?" I began to pull out those things that would apply to me and help me in my life. That is how I began to read the Word of God.

Now, there are plans for your daily Bible reading. You can get books at a Christian bookstore to help you read through the Bible in one year, a calendar. But let me encourage you, I did not understand everything when I began reading it. I would sit down. I was a mommy and I was tired. I had to get up early in the morning and if I sat down to read, sometimes I would go back to sleep. I would take my Bible and walk very quietly and read it out loud. Little did I know the principle that faith comes by hearing, and as I read out loud, it began to get down on the inside of me. Then I began to hear it more and it began to come up out of me. It began to change my attitude. It began to change my mind. It began to change my life.

I also read *The Authority of the Believer* and *Prevailing Prayer to Peace* by Kenneth E. Hagin. I took books that were on the specific subjects and I studied those subjects. I believe the Holy Spirit will help you to do this. I would read books, but I wouldn't take the book as the final authority. I would check the Bible to make sure it was the final word. And if I found something I did not understand or I did not think was right, I just put it on the shelf and left it there.

Sometimes the Holy Spirit would prompt me to get it back off the shelf when I was ready to learn from it. And sometimes I never did get it off the shelf because not all books line up with Bible truths. Don't let anyone's book be "gospel." Verify everything you read with the Bible.

That is the way I began to read the Word of God, and I tell you, it is wonderful. I cannot get enough of it. It is a whole book of, "Yes, we can do this. We can do that. We will overcome. Yes, this is the answer as to what I need to do."

When I have a problem or a situation, I just sit down and say, "Holy Spirit, the Scripture says You were left here to instruct me and show me the way. I need to know what to do with this situation." Then, I begin to leaf through my Bible and the next thing I know, I have a revelation. I will know exactly how to handle that situation.

The Holy Spirit will teach you well. He is a good teacher. You need to learn to read your Bible and even if you find it boring to start out, you will begin to find it means life to you if you will read it out loud.

If you just begin to read it out of obedience, the Holy Spirit will begin to teach you.

Checklist for Priorities

What do you tend to make the most important in your life? Your children, homemaking, appearance, money, security, wife's parents, careers, or talents? That is only to give you a checkup as to what is most important in your life. The point I am trying to make is that sometimes all of these things I have listed become more important than our relationship with God and our relationship with our husband. I did not list husbands, but our relationship with our husband is very important. So let me encourage you to line up priorities.

I will tell you how I used to line up my priorities:

Number 1 - Children.
Number 2 - Homemaking and keeping my house clean.
Number 3 - My appearance because I worked.
Number 4 - Money and security.
Number 5 - My parents.

I put everything ahead of my husband. The career I had and my talents were more important to me at that time. I didn't know I was doing wrong, but when I checked my attitude, those were the things that were priorities to me. There was no time for my relationship with God or with my husband.

Do you feel good with yourself as a wife, a mother, a homemaker, and a career woman?

This will give you an analysis of how you feel. Do you feel like the spiritual leader in your family? How many women have felt that way? Let me talk to you about it. I felt the same way.

I was the one who brought all the spiritual things to the household. So one day my husband had left for work and I was praying about it. I said, "God, I am teaching women (I was teaching at that time) that their husbands are to be the spiritual leader of the household, yet I do not feel that is the way in our household and I am not going to be a hypocrite. I am past playing games. If we can't make it happen in our household, then I am not going to teach anymore."

The Holy Spirit said to me, "Proverbs 31:15." At that time, I had taught this enough that I knew it line upon line. I said, "God, I know what Proverbs 31 says. I have memorized it line upon line." I sat there and I kept hearing, "Proverbs 31:15." I have a relationship with the Father that I just talk to Him, so I said, "I'll show You that I know what Proverbs 31:15 says." And I began to read, **"She rises while it is yet night and gets [spiritual] food for her household and assigns her maids their tasks."**

The Spirit of the Lord said to me, "In the same way you prepare your physical food, you prepare your spiritual food for your household. The only difference is your attitude." Then God said, "You think you are the spiritual leader because you are giving all the spiritual food, but the Word tells you to get spiritual food for your household. If you change your attitude, your husband will then take his place."

> A change in your attitude will change the atmosphere in your home.

My attitude changed. I served him spiritual food, and I served him physical food. Out of that I began to watch him grow, to begin to change, and then he became the pastor of Cornerstone Church in Grove, Oklahoma.

It is your attitude, ladies. You may be the one bringing spiritual food, but the Word of God says, "She rises while it is yet night." I know that from the Holy Spirit. I had never read about attitude in any book, but I began to bring my husband spiritual food, served on a silver platter. I began to read to him when we would go on trips, and I would begin to feed him spiritually until his appetite became so great towards spiritual things that he began to read. He did not have to take just bites. He could take whole plates full, and he got to the point where he was getting his own spiritual food.

Prayer

Father, I pray for the ladies who have read chapter 5 regarding the inner and outer beauty of the woman, because it may seem overwhelming to them, seeing the list of challenges needed to be the person You want them to be.

Holy Spirit, open their eyes to see not a list of do's and don'ts, but to see the blessings You have promised if they pattern their lives according to the model You have given.

If any lady is feeling overwhelmed right now, reveal to her that You are her help and guide, and You go before her to make the crooked places straight.

If any would say, "I can't change, I was born that way. All of my family are that way," I ask that this lie of the devil be destroyed in Jesus' name.

I pray that every lady will be so excited about the blessings You have promised that they will make every effort to conform to Your Word, so they can say with Paul, "I press toward the mark of the high calling of God in Christ Jesus."

I ask these things in Jesus' name. Amen.

Nuggets from Chapter 5

Proverbs 31:28-30 states:

Her children rise up and call her blessed, (happy, fortunate, and to be envied); and her husband boasts of and praises her, [saying],

Many daughters have done virtuously, nobly, and well [with the strength of character that is steadfast in goodness], but you excel them all.

Charm and grace are deceptive, and beauty is vain [because it is not lasting], but a woman who reverently and worshipfully fears the Lord, she shall be praised!

I want to give you some comments from *The Amplified Bible* regarding these verses.

"Many daughters have done . . . nobly, and well . . . but you excel them all." There is a great deal to be recorded of her – a woman in private life. It means she has done more than Miriam, the leader of a nation's women in praise to God (Exodus 15:20,21); Deborah, the patriotic military advisor (Judges 4:4-10); Huldah, the woman who revealed God's secret message to national leaders (2 Kings 22:14); Ruth, the woman of constancy (Ruth 1:16); Hannah, the ideal mother (1 Samuel 1:20, 2:19); the Shunammite, the hospitable woman (2 Kings 4:8-10), and even more than Queen Esther, the woman who risked sacrificing her life for her people (Esther 4:16).

In what way did she excel them all? In her spiritual and practical devotion to God, that permeated every area and relationship of her life. All seven of the Christian virtues listed in Second Peter 1:5-7 are there *like colored threads in a tapestry.*

Her secret, which is open to everyone, is the Holy Spirit's climax of the story and of this book. In verse 30, to reverently and worshipfully fear the Lord is the principal part of wisdom (Proverbs 1:7). The woman is given the full responsibility for a life that is valued by God and by her husband, as **"far above rubies or pearls"** (Proverbs 31:10).

Now, I am going to ask you about your assignments. The first one was to write twenty good things about yourself. I trust that you have completed it. Now, take the list, fold it, and put it someplace where you can check it again when you are really down and have blown it. Take that list out and read it again to remind yourself how valuable and precious you are.

Then, you were to memorize Psalm 139:14 TLB. It says, **"Thank you for making me so wonderfully complex!"** We have to know that we are God's creation. We did not have anything to do with forming ourselves. God said He knew us before we were formed in the womb of our mothers. He charted every day of our life. He says He has us tattooed on the palms of His hands and our lives are continually before Him (Isaiah 49:16).

The price you pay for something is what it is worth, and the price that was paid for you was the precious blood of Jesus. That means you are worth a lot. That is the reason he says, **"Thank you for making me so wonderfully complex! It is amazing to think about . . ."** (Proverbs 139:14 TLB).

I think about Janet Lay, my life, the things that God has done in my life, the way He created me and fashioned me in my mother's womb with ears that hear, eyes that see, a nose that smells, a brain that thinks, and a body that walks and functions. He did all that. I didn't. *Thank You, heavenly Father. Your workmanship on Janet Lay is marvelous and how well I know it.* That is not pride and it is not ego, because everything I have is a gift from God.

A lot of times you put yourself down, and you talk about yourself like you are a gift from someplace else. God doesn't like for you to talk about His kids. So, do not say negative things about yourself. If you

122

have not made your list of twenty things and memorized Psalm 139:14 TLB, be sure to do it, because it will help you change your attitude.

You were to make a list of at least ten good things about your mate and give it to him. You might need to make a carbon copy so you can remind yourself sometimes when you are looking to the negative side. Also, the "look" signs you made will help remind you of his good qualities. Let me tell you, a good place to put one is over your telephone. I have had one over my telephone for many years, and if I get a negative report, it reminds me to look to the person's good side.

Philippians 4:8 says to think on things that are true, honest, just, pure, lovely, and of good report. Put one on your mirror, and it will remind you to look to your good side.

Then, you were to ask your husband for three things he would like for you to change. A lot of times they do not want to share those things with you. When I asked Bill for the three things, he would not give them to me. But then I said, "Honey, I am really trying to become a better wife." Then he gave me his list of the three things. You have to be careful about your reaction once they share with you. If you respond in a negative sense, they will not share with you again. If it is a closed subject, then you make your own list.

> "But as it is written, Eye hath not seen, nor ear heard, neither have entered into the heart of man, the things which God hath prepared for them that love him"
>
> (1 Corinthians 2:9 kjv).

CHAPTER 6

The Art of Good Homemaking

Lord, I want to do something for You.
What? Wash the dishes!

The art of good homemaking really sounds spiritual, doesn't it?
Let me tell you, when we get through the lesson in this chapter,
you will realize how important it is.

Our Homes Are Very Important

As a review, I took the title of this course, *The Fragrance of
Knowledge,* from Second Corinthians 2:14,15:

> But thanks be to God, Who in Christ always leads us in
> triumph [as trophies of Christ's victory] and through us
> spreads and makes evident the fragrance of the knowledge of
> God everywhere,
> For we are the sweet fragrance of Christ [which exhales]
> unto God, [discernible alike] among those who are being saved
> and among those who are perishing.

As women, I believe we have the blessing of becoming that sweet-smelling fragrance in whatever situation we are in – among those who are perishing and those who are not. The reason I wrote this course is that the Holy Spirit instructed me that He wanted me to go and teach and cause *women to stand up and know that they are winners in life.* And with that attitude, they become sweet-smelling fragrances wherever they go. Then I began to teach Proverbs 31:10-31, about the virtuous woman line upon line.

The text for this chapter is from Proverbs 31:27: **"She looks well to how things go in her household, and the bread of idleness (gossip, discontent, and self-pity) she will not eat."**

When it says she will not eat, it is like someone sets food down in front of you that you know is not good for you, and you make a choice whether to eat it or not. So idleness, gossip, discontent, and self-pity are breads that you have the opportunity to eat. *The choice is up to you.*

There are times when I really do not want to do something in my house, but I get myself by the nape of the neck and I do it. I believe that there are times when you should be able to sit down on your couch and be at peace and have reading times. Of course, you have your time with the Lord. I believe in reading good books and things that feed us emotionally along with spiritual books. I never get tired of reading things about my home and ways to minister and to be keepers in the home.

Titus 2:4,5 says that as an older woman, I am to teach younger women to love their husbands and to be keepers in the home. The same Word of God that tells us to go into all nations and preach in different places also tells us that as mature women (I like "mature" better than "older"!), we have a responsibility, not just the person who is doing the teaching, to teach the younger women. Every one of us know someone whom we can disciple and teach, meeting the needs in their life.

126

Do not think that just because you are younger that you do not have something to give, because everyone has something to give. You may be older in your spirit than another person.

It is not enough just to win one, you should also teach one. Everyone needs to be taught so it is very important that you do not eat the bread of idleness because you have a job to do.

Proverbs 31 says that the virtuous woman reaches out her filled hands to the needy. *The Amplified Bible* says "whether in mind, body, or spirit." Whatever the need is, she reaches out. She has something to give.

> My goal in this chapter is to help you have a different attitude regarding your home.

This does not mean a woman who has always done everything right and doesn't have any regrets because of past mistakes. But it does mean a woman who has believed in her heart and confessed with her mouth that Jesus died for her sins and all her past is wiped clean. She is now a virtuous woman.

It goes on to say that she looks *well* to how things go in her household, whether it be one room or ten. If you are single or married, you have a place you live so you should look well to your household. I think single women need to learn this because when you live by yourself, sometimes you have the lack of motivation and not really care how things are because you are the only person living there.

You need to think enough of yourself – that is the reason I start out teaching on who you are in Christ Jesus – that you keep your house smelling good, looking good, and feeling good for you, as that is your place of refuge, your place of shelter. *So our homes are very important.* I believe that if our homes were not important, it would not have been mentioned in Proverbs.

Again, Proverbs 31:27 says, **"She looks well to how things go in her household, and the bread of idleness (gossip, discontent, and self-pity) she will not eat."** You need to write these four words down and make it a goal in your life that you will not eat of them. You are not

127

going to eat the bread of gossip. You are not going to eat the bread of idleness. You are not going to eat the bread of discontent – never being content with what you have.

A lot of people are still pressing on for what they are going to get and they do not enjoy what they have, so they stay discontented all the time. God wants us to enjoy what He has given us. I believe if we are faithful over the little things and enjoy the little things, then He allows us to have more things. *He does not want things to have us, but it is okay for us to have things.*

You are not going to eat the bread of self-pity. In the past I had enough pity parties for a lifetime. The only thing I ever found out about pity parties is that they make you feel worse. I remember the last pity party I had, and when I made that decision, I realized that it didn't hurt anyone but me. My husband did not act any different, and my kids did not act any different.

I used to sit on my front porch and cry when my husband went to work and say, "Oh, God, why did I marry someone who worked nights? We can't be a normal family like other people. Everybody else is having dinner and they are going places together. Not only does he sleep late on Sunday mornings because he works until 6:00 a.m., but he cannot go to church and I have to go sit by myself. Boo hoo hoo!" I have done all those things.

I looked at other people and saw how good they had it, not knowing that maybe they did not have it as good as I did. And when you compare yourself with other people, it sets you up for a pity party. Be blessed with what you have and enjoy it.

When I look at Proverbs 31:10-31, I think there is no way in the natural that you can do all the things which are mentioned, but in the supernatural you can. That is what I want you to know in studying this chapter: *There is more strength and power within you than you realize, because you have Jesus in you, the hope of glory.* When you have Jesus in you, you can do a lot of things. He will make your feet lighter.

Not only that, His yoke is easy and His burden is light (see Matthew 11:30 KJV).

I want to tell you, a lot of times your attitude is heavier on you than the work you have to do. Because if you have the right attitude, you are looking for things to be thankful for. A lot of times you get in that other realm looking at things you don't have for which to be thankful. When your attitude is right, you will find your work a lot easier than it would be with the weight of a bad attitude.

The story is told about Sir Christopher Wren, the architect who built St. Paul's Cathedral, where he had some workers building the cathedral for him. He went on the job site one day. Several laborers were working. He went to one man and said, "What are you doing?" He said, "I am just breaking this pile of rocks." He went to another man and said, "What are you doing?" He replied, "I am building a building for Sir Christopher Wren." He went to the third worker and asked him, "What are you doing?" He said, "I am building a cathedral to God." All were doing the same thing, but with different attitudes. Who do you think was enjoying his work? The one who was building a cathedral for God.

The word "wife" was taken from the root word "weaver." You weave into the home the atmosphere of love, joy, peace, and longsuffering, or discontent and self-pity. I am sure you already realize that the attitude you have in your home usually is the same attitude that everyone else has. You probably have heard men joke, "If Mama is not happy, nobody is happy."

I remember one evening after my husband had gone to work, I took my boys to a place in Tulsa where we had hot dogs for dinner. I guess there was something wrong with the chili, because after we got home, all four of my sons and I were sick. We only had one bathroom and we were in a mess. I had never asked my husband over two or three times to come home from work. I called him and said, "Honey, I need you to come home." I told him what happened. He came in the front door and took one look. Remember, he did not go to dinner with us, but he got sick.

I always found that when I got sick, the household got sick. Whatever attitude I had, my children would pick up. If I was grumpy, they would be grumpy. My husband would come home and he would be grumpy too. *So you have the opportunity to set the atmosphere in your home.*

It is very important what you let come into your home in the daytime. Be careful what program is on your television. Through your television come spirits that you would not let come in through your front door. If a person like those on television would knock on your door and you knew that there was perversion or other negative traits, you would not open the front door and you would not let the person in the door. Yet, with one little turn or push of the button, if you are not careful, you let all kinds of spirits come into your home.

I encourage you to keep Christian music or the Word of God playing. I have often felt if someone got into my home when I wasn't there and I had the Christian station on, they would hear about God in my home. They are not going to hang around long. So a good protection is to leave good music playing, even if it goes over and over again. It will set a good atmosphere.

When we began to put our home in order, we had a young man who lived two doors from us. We had been neighbors for several years. He was the same age as one of our sons. One of the things I quit doing was screaming and yelling at my children. I would get loud with my kids all day long. About three o'clock they got in serious trouble because they had pressed me all day. So we had this strife, this bawling, carrying on, and this yelling woman going on in our house all the time.

I watched my husband as we began to put things in order and he told me, "Why don't you just tell them one time? If they don't do it, then take care of them." I watched and that is what he did.

I went to my children – not in a time of discipline – and told them that I had been wrong. I called my boys around me and I told them from that time on, I would only tell them one time. I said, "I will make sure you hear me." For the younger children, I would have them repeat it back so that later in the day they could not say, "Mama, you didn't tell me that." *Children are precious, but they are not innocent.*

I learned that if there was any doubt that they heard and understood me, as I was responsible for good communication, I would look them in the eyes and tell them one time. If I felt that I needed to, I would have them repeat back so that I was sure they were understanding. Then, if they did not do it, there was discipline, and I didn't keep telling them a dozen times. I tell you, that one little tool caused our house to settle down and there was such a peaceful atmosphere in it.

Back to the little boy next door. Monty was probably eleven. He came over to our house one day and I had the television turned off and I had music playing. The yelling and hollering had settled down and

> Women have the ability to set the atmosphere in their home.

the discipline was in order. Monty just stood there looking around. I said, "What's wrong, Monty?" "Well," he said, "you have redecorated or something. There is something different in your house." Before God, we had not done one physical thing to our house. It was the atmosphere in our home which was different.

If your children are gone, you still need to take care of the atmosphere in your home and make sure that your home is a place of peace, love, and joy, a place that your husband is happy to come home to.

I never drive into my driveway and into my garage that I am not thankful to be home. When we make a trip, always when I get home – no matter how far it is or how wonderful it is – I am always glad to be home. I say, "Oh, it is so good to be home." Why? That is my little nest that God has given me. I know what it is to have a little nest, a medium-sized nest, and a large nest. But when I had my little nest, I took care of it the same way that I take care of my big nest. So regardless of where you live, it's your little nest, and you need to take care of it with the abilities God has given you. So our attitude is very important.

How To Get Your House in Order

The most important rule for success in homemaking is found in Ecclesiastes 3:1 KJV which says, **"To every thing there is a season, and a time to every purpose under the heaven."** In other words, there is a time for everything.

A lot of times you might think that working in your home long hours is taking care of your home. It never hurts to have outside help if that is what you desire. Or, you might think it is doing the most important things first. If you work very fast, that helps. That is okay, but that is not the rule for success in homemaking.

I want to stop here and share that a lot of times in my time frame, I realize that I do not have time to do everything I need to do. Especially before we moved from Tulsa, Oklahoma, I traveled a lot. I would have a plane to catch. I would have a meeting to do, and I knew I had to be ready by a certain time. I had a lot of things to do because I really try to practice what I preach. If I tell you to leave your homes in order, I leave my home in order. I do not try to tell women things that I am not trying to put into my own life.

I would pray and say, "Holy Spirit, I need Your help in getting this done." And you know what? I do not know if angels were helping me or what happened, but I would get done and have time left over. It was like the clock moved slower. I have checked the clock to see if it was still running, because I accomplished so much. So don't think you are on your own when you are doing your work. *The Holy Spirit will help you.* You have the angels of the Lord encamped round about you, and they will help you get things done supernaturally. I cannot tell you how, but they do.

The answer to getting your home in order – the goal, the purpose, the rule – is to organize your time and priorities. Now, before you set your goal or plans, you need to know what you want, so let me give you four words that will help in your planning.

1. *Purpose.* What is your purpose today? To be at Bible study on time, or to have order in your home by noon? Whatever your purpose is today, that is what you do.

2. *Goal.* What is your goal today, your accomplishment?[11] Are you going to call someone? Are you going to mop the kitchen floor?

I realize you are only setting guidelines and that every day brings new opportunities to overcome. That is okay. If you have a goal to reach, if you have something to reach for, it will keep you from being idle and waking up every morning in a new world. Have you ever done that? Like, "What am I going to do today?"

3. *Priorities.* It is very important to line up priorities. I make a list of things that I need to do, and then I number them. Most important, number 1, number 2, number 3, number 4, and number 5. I may not get numbers 4 and 5 done, but 1, 2, and 3 get done. So, that will help you.

4. *Planning.* Start planning and then make plans to accomplish your goal.

There are two robbers of our time and energy, which are worry and diversion of our attention.

I understand that some of us are not as young as others and do not have the energy that we had when we were sixteen. The Bible does tell us, however, in Psalm 92:13,14 KJV:

> Purpose – Goal
> – Priorities –
> Planning

Those that be planted in the house of the Lord shall flourish in the courts of our God.
They shall still bring forth fruit in old age; they shall be fat and flourishing.

---

[11] Dr. Thernos York says, "Have realistic goals (1 Timothy 4:4). Ask, 'Is it a worthy goal?' and set a time limit. Work out each goal one at a time. God will never hold you responsible to complete what you are incapable of." Dr. York also says, "Decide deliberately to make your goal and to overcome circumstances."

Verse 14 in *The Amplified Bible reads,* "[Growing in grace] they shall still bring forth fruit in old age; they shall be full of sap [of spiritual vitality] and [rich in the] verdure [of trust, love, and contentment]."

You can choose to get old, I believe, or you can choose to use your energy. There are days when I have to make my energy be more than it wants to be, and I try to be wise in those things. But I believe your energy will grow as you use it.

A woman can find happiness in homemaking by treating her home like her ministry.

A lot of ladies tell me, "I have the same old beds to be made, same laundry to be done every Monday, I wash the same sheets, I wash the same underwear, towels, washcloths, and I do the same dishes. I cook in the same pots and pans. I sweep the same floor. I clean the same bathroom." I have had women say, "It is drudgery, the same old thing. Why not leave the bed unmade? We are going to get back in it." *Drudgery!*

The attitude you need to have is found in Colossians 3:23,24 KJV:

> **And whatsoever ye do, do it heartily, as to the Lord, and not unto men;**
> **Knowing that of the Lord ye shall receive the reward of the inheritance: for ye serve the Lord Christ.**

What makes the difference is your attitude toward homemaking. Colossians 3:17 KJV says, **"And whatsoever ye do in word or deed, do all in the name of the Lord Jesus. . . ."** Is homemaking a deed? You need to treat your homemaking like a ministry unto the Lord. It is just as important for me to minister in my home and keep it in order as it is for me to study and teach Bible study.

A few years ago when we were in Tulsa, I began to notice an attitude in Christian women's circles. There was an attitude that took on almost the same spirit as the Equal Rights Movement when women became very independent. I really prayed about it. I thought, *Lord, maybe I have taught wrong, because I have taught that women are equally as important as men, but are functionally different.* God made us that way. It is not that I think women are second-class citizens. No! In fact, I think we are extra first-class citizens. I want women to know that. But I think there is an attitude that we can get of being so independent that it makes the men feel that there is no need for them.

I prayed, "Lord, if I have taught this wrong, I will go back and correct it." And I got my answer from the Holy Spirit who reminded me of what I taught back in Genesis about Eve when Satan tempted her to eat of the fruit of the tree. It was not because she was hungry or needed food, because she had plenty of food. But Satan told her if she ate of the tree she would be like God and she would know good or evil. It had to do with position and control for God was in control. So that is what she was tempted with: *control and position.*

I went ahead and kept my firm stand, kept teaching the same thing while hearing other women speaking things in the wrong attitude about their husbands in the pulpit, the attitude being, "I want my position." A person's gift will make room for them (Proverbs 18:16). You do not have to have the title to have the position. When you want the title and you are working for a title, usually you lose the position. You control out of fear and by having that independent attitude.

One day I was teaching my Victory Bible Institute class, and I made this statement. It may shock some of you. It shocked me when it came out of my mouth. I do not know whether it was flesh or God, but it sure sounded good when I got it out there. I said, "Who says it is more spiritual to cast out a devil than it is to sweep the floor? The Word of God says, 'Whatever you do (pray, lay hands on the sick, sweep the floor), do everything as unto the Lord.'" It is in your attitude.

So I am saying to you that there is to be a ministry attitude in your home because God placed you there. Remember when Jesus told the people to go out and preach the gospel, He said, **"In Jerusalem, and in all Judaea, and in Samaria, and unto the uttermost part of the earth."**[12]

135

Jerusalem was where they were. I call your home "Jerusalem," and then you can go to Samaria and wherever you need to go. But to leave our homes unkempt, having the attitude that your home is unimportant, is letting your Jerusalem be uncared for. And I really find to be a success in ministry, careers, or whatever you are doing, you have to keep an attitude that your home is important and that there is a ministry there. Titus 2:4,5 doesn't tell me to teach you a lot of other things, but it does tell me to teach women how to be keepers at home.

Basic Steps for Having an Orderly House

Colossians 3:17 says, **"And whatever you do [no matter what it is] in word or deed, do everything in the name of the Lord Jesus and in [dependence upon] His Person, giving praise to God the Father through Him."**

A good attitude starts with gratitude. Thank God for dirty dishes. That means you have food to eat. Thank God for dirty clothes to wash. That means you have something to wear. Thank God for a house to clean. That means you have a place to live. Thank God for dirty socks on the floor. That means a man lives there.

I want to share with you four basic steps for having an orderly house.

1. *Make your bed.* It isn't real spiritual, but the first thing you are to do when you come out of your bed is to make it. Now, if you have a husband who is in it, don't make it over him! The reason I say that is, my husband was a night worker for probably eighteen years, so he was always in bed in the morning. I would have to get up and close the bedroom door very quietly. Sometimes before I learned better, I closed it loudly because I wanted him to get up. He tells about the first Sunday I came home from church and didn't slam everything in an attempt to get him out of bed.

---

[12] Acts 1:8 KJV - **"But ye shall receive power, after that the Holy Ghost is come upon you: and ye shall be witnesses unto me both in Jerusalem, and in all Judaea, and in Samaria, and unto the uttermost part of the earth."**

2. *Do your dishes.* If you do not have a dishwasher, make a sink of soapy water to put your dishes in while you are cooking. Thank God for dirty dishes. That means you have food to eat.

3. *Wipe your bathrooms.* Don't scrub them, just wipe with a clean cloth, wipe your dressing table and your stool. If you raise four boys and you have a husband in the house, you know the stool needs to be wiped. Don't get into deep cleaning. If you do these things before you get into deep cleaning, the house will be in order.

4. *Pick up your clutter.* Everything in your house should have a place to live. You say, "Now, you just don't understand. That is not possible." Yes, I do understand!

I had a wonderful experience with a couple before I was writing the course. This was while we were still at Sheridan Christian Center, Tulsa, Oklahoma. This couple had just come to Jesus, and they had lived under a bridge in Tulsa. They had one little child. The church put them on staff as maintenance people for provision and rented a place for them to live. We got them a mattress, box springs, and a few things for the house, but there were no chest of drawers or place for their clothes.

As I counseled the lady, I realized that she had not been taught how to take care of her house. They started being late for work at the church every day, and Pastor asked me to get them in and find out why they couldn't get to work on time, so we called them in. The problem was that she would do her laundry, but she had no drawers or storage places. She would bring the laundry back, didn't fold it, and left it in piles, because no one had ever trained her. So they couldn't find their clothes a lot of times in the morning because everything was such a mess with no planning.

So we went to the grocery store and got cardboard boxes. We took a marker and wrote on one box, "Joey's clothes." We folded his underwear and socks and put them in the box. We had a box saying, "Paul's clothes" and "Nancy's clothes." We organized her house with cardboard boxes.

Now, ladies, everything in your house should have a place to live. If in doubt, toss it out. Don't throw your husband's things away. If he has got that little ring around his chair, just fold his papers and respect his right to leave them right there. He needs his little area. Do the best you can, but I encourage you to pick up your clutter.

Clutter should be picked up the night before. Children should be taught to put things where they belong. If you are messy, don't expect your children not to be messy because they will be. You say, "Well, mine are too young."

Here is what a three-year-old child can do daily before breakfast: Dress, put their pajamas away, brush their teeth, wash their face, brush their hair, make the bed with help, and tidy up their bedroom. After lunch: They can clear the lunch table, help load the dishwasher, and then take a nap. I believe all small children need a time out. If they don't, Mother sure does. If they don't want to go to sleep, then give them a book and put them on their bed for an hour. They need this and you need it. Before story time or bedtime, they can pick up toys and prepare for bed. Weekly before play, empty wastebaskets (a three year old can empty wastebaskets), help in the garden and little flower beds. They can pull weeds in an assigned area of the yard.

How much strength does it take to go out and pick up papers or do something in the yard? When necessary, help to clean the closets and straighten up the drawers. That is a three year old. You say, "That is not realistic."

Let me tell you about an experience I had when I was teaching in Kansas. I met a couple who had adopted a three-year-old child from a foreign country who had been in an orphanage. They were shocked when they brought the three year old and set the child beside their three-year-old natural child at the table. This child would come in, get a hanger, and put her coat on it. Their child would come in and throw hers on the floor.

Don't underestimate your children. Don't wait for them to get old enough to do things. They need to be taught to help. You take their little hands and you pick the toy up and put it where it belongs so they will know.

A five-year-old child: Before breakfast they can dress, put their pajamas away, brush their teeth, wash their face, comb their hair, make their bed, and with occasional help, tidy up their room before play. After breakfast they can load the dishwasher, clean up the kitchen, clean the television screen and bedroom furniture. Before lunch: Put things away and set the table. After lunch: A quiet time – reading, games, etc. Before story time and bedtime: Pick up toys. Sometimes it is nice to have a little reward for the one who gets their toys picked up first or gets their room cleaned up first.

Let your children help. If you try to do it all yourself, you will get worn out. It helps them to be part of the family, and you are teaching them to be diligent.

Grocery Shopping

Grocery shopping is good homemaking. The most important thing in grocery shopping is not necessarily having your husband go with you, but it is making out your menus before you go to the store so you will know what items you need. Don't go to the grocery store when you are hungry. You will overspend. About twelve or fifteen years ago, I received some statistics, and at that time it cost 76 cents for every minute you were in the grocery store. (Today it is probably four times that much.) So I am saying you need to make out your menus and your list.

I believe in coupons, but they can cause impulsive buying. Don't buy something just because you have a coupon for it. Only buy if it is on your list. A lot of pantries are full of stuff that you don't need.

Making out menus may seem hard to you. You don't have to say Monday, Tuesday, Wednesday, etc., but make the list for four or five meals before you go to the grocery store. Get the newspaper on Thursday and check the ads. Whatever store has the most things on sale that are on your list, go to that store. Shop where they have the most items on sale or where the prices are right. It is important to shop stores that have sales on things you want, and you will learn to be a frugal shopper.[13]

How To Organize Your Time

One of the books I read which helped me to organize my time was *Sidetracked Home Executives* by Wanette Crystal. I learned from this book to do priority things first: Make your bed, wipe your bathrooms, do your dishes, and pick up your clutter. Then do your closets and then your extra activities.

Don't dump everything on the floor. You never know who is coming for dinner, especially if you are the Pastor's wife. If you will do those four things, though, you won't care who rings your doorbell. If you spend all day cleaning the pantry and cleaning your closets, but you haven't done your four things, no one is going to appreciate your pantry and closets when they come to your house. You will want to go to the door and say, "Look at my clean closets."

I understand that Phyllis Diller at one time had some get-well cards that she put on her mantle so if her house had not been cleaned, people would think she had been sick.

Enjoy your role as a homemaker. If you don't, you need to change your attitude.

Enjoy Your Role as a Mother

One of our sons comes to our home on weekends and stays with us. He has to leave the house about six o'clock because he works in Tulsa. He has his alarm set at 5:15 or 5:30. Usually, I get him something hot to drink. On one particular Monday morning, he was ready to leave. I had hardly got him out the door until he was back again.

---

[13] Proverbs 31:16 - **"She considers a [new] field** (or groceries) **before she buys or accepts it . . . with her savings [of time and strength] she plants fruitful vines in her vineyard** (or food in her pantry)."

He didn't have any car keys. So, with a mother's intuition I began praying in the Spirit, "We need the car keys. We need the car keys." We looked every place. I had him go get his luggage, and we began going through it on the living room floor. I am praying in the Spirit all the time. "Angels, help us find the car keys so he won't be late for work."

You know, he is human, like his mother, and sometimes we do not put our car keys where we need to put them. But I said to him, "Son, you were standing here at the kitchen bar last night and you were talking to your father about a bill in town you needed to pay and you gave him the money. By chance, would your keys be in your billfold?" He pulled his billfold out of his pocket, opened it up, and there were his car keys.

You never get over being a mother. As your children get older and leave the household, you have to be careful of the counsel you give them. They do not always want our counsel. Sometimes we have to pray and let God be God in their lives. But you never get over being a mother, and I am grateful that I am a mother.

I have four wonderful sons and two beautiful daughters-in-love. I do not say my sons have always made my heart glad, but I still thank God that I am a mother. You know, I think God must have known the kind of children that I would need and that is what He gave me. And He must have known the areas of my life that would be strengthened through children. They have taught me a lot, but I thank God they have kept me on my knees praying so my prayer life is better. I know about answered prayer. I know about speaking the Word of God, which I might not have known if I did not have children. So I enjoy my role as a mother – raising, teaching, and loving.

There comes a time when you have to love them and release them and let God be God in their life. You just trust God. You get a vision and don't see them any other way except that they are serving God. I don't care what they are doing or what they are not doing. You have to keep that vision before you so that you can treat them like they are already serving the Lord. Do not treat them like sinners. They are the seed of the righteous and delivered from all destruction, and that is all we need to see them as. So enjoy your role as a mother.

What Is a Capable and Independent Woman?

It sounds good to be a capable and independent woman. I am not talking about killing your own snakes. I am talking about being so independent you never need your husband's help. When I started getting my life and home in order, I had four sons. I mowed the lawn; I did everything. One of the reasons was that they never could do it to please me. But you know what? I began to back off and not be so independent. I resigned from mowing the lawn.

There was a lady in our class in Tulsa, Oklahoma, who at one time had been a truck driver before she married, so she knew a lot about doing things mechanically. One of the three things her husband wanted was for her to be more feminine, so we told her she needed to resign from doing some things and she did. She quit changing the oil in her car. Now, I am not telling you not to do it if you do, but she did quit.

One day she set the oil in the living room. Her husband didn't change it. Finally he said to her, "When are you going to change the oil in the car?" She said, "I resigned that, remember?" He said, "You know how to change the oil, so you had better get it done." She just took it out there and made a mess of it, pouring oil all over everything. So he said to her, "Why did you do that?" She said, "Well, it is very difficult for me to be feminine and be changing the oil in my car at the same time."

I realize when you are single, a lot of times you have to do some of these things. I am just saying that if you are married, you need to let your husband know you need him. I ask my husband to do things for me. They don't always notice, but when you are so independent that you do everything yourself, they don't see any need to help you.

So, I encourage you to let your husband do things for you. Let your sons do things for you. Step back and let them. A lot of times we take over the masculine chores.

If you do have a masculine job, do it in a feminine manner. Keep a bow in your hair. I am serious. When we first started teaching on the family, we taught in the farm communities. I told the women to do something feminine. Put lace on their jeans. Wear some earrings. Do something so there is a difference between the man and the woman. You will be treated differently if you will dress differently.

I have always told our single girls, "I know jeans are popular. I wear them. You wear them. But I want to tell you something. When you have a dress on, you get treated differently by men than when you are in jeans."

When girls go on a date, they need to dress more feminine. The boys will be more respectful of them if they dress more feminine. I am not against jeans. I have them in my closet. I love them. I wore them to a football game and my husband told me, "I like you in your jeans." There is nothing wrong with jeans, but there is a time when you need to be a little more feminine even if it means a pair of earrings or a little bow or the way you walk.

The world was not complete until we got here. God put you here and He made you a woman, so what I am saying is just to remember you are a woman. Then you will be surprised at the treatment you will get.

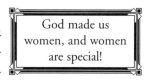

God made us women, and women are special!

Killing Your Own Snakes

The other day someone was at our house, standing in our foyer. Remember, I raised four boys so I've killed spiders, I have found frogs in their pockets, snakes in my house, and I am not afraid of those things. But I do not need to always kill my own snakes.

Bill was standing in the foyer talking with the visitor, and there was a spider crawling up the wall. They were talking about the spider. As I came around the corner, I saw the spider crawling up the wall. With my husband standing there, I just reached up, knocked the spider down, put my foot on it, and that was the end of it. Then I began thinking, *There you go, killing your own snakes. Your husband was standing there. Why didn't you let him take care of it?* We can kill those snakes, but I encourage you to be a little more feminine. Let your husband change the flat tire.

Do You Need Your Husband's Protection?

You need to check yourself. Yes, we do need them. See, they have been created to be a protector. They are the lover, leader, protector, and provider. If you do not need their protection, there is a role in their life that is not being fulfilled.

How does a woman make a man feel when she can take care of herself? She makes him feel unmasculine. Do you work outside the home? Is there a need for you to work? I believe that if women need to go to work and help with the finances, then the husband and children should help her in her role as a homemaker. It is a shared responsibility.

If you work outside the home, is it because you are trying to escape from the home? When you work eight or ten hours on a job, it is very difficult to do some of the things I have been talking about. I recognize that. I know what it is to work outside the home. I also know that all the time I worked outside my home, I did it because I wanted a few more things. But by the time you pay for your child care, your clothing, your lunch and fast food dinners, I wonder how much you really get to take home.[14] Is it worth it?

Do not let work be an escape from home. I have had women tell me, "I do not like housework." Well, you need to change your attitude. God said it is He who works to will and do His good pleasure. If He gave us the assignment to be keepers in our home, then I believe

144

that we need to take care of the assignment He gave us. I am not telling you not to work. I am asking you to check your motive to see why you are working.

Are you working to help your husband? Great. I have had many jobs to make extra money. I have done a lot of things to supplement the income, but don't let work outside the home be an escape from your home. Some ladies would love to stay home and if you are blessed enough to get to stay home, then take care of it and enjoy your role.

Some ladies have husbands who do not think the wife can stay home because of finances. If that is your situation, when you get a vacation you make sure the dinner smells good when he comes home in the evening. Have his slippers setting out for him so he will see the difference in your being home or out working eight or ten hours a day, and he will start figuring out a way where you can stay home.

Before I quit working outside the home, I would drive through South Tulsa on the way home from the doctor's office where I worked. I would think, *Lord, someday You are going to let me have a lovely new home.* And I thought I was working toward that goal. Do you know when I got my first new home? When I quit my job and started staying home. God began to promote my husband, began to bless him, and we built our first new home. So God can do it if we will just get our attitudes right regarding what we are supposed to do.

I know I am touching on some sensitive areas in this chapter, but I have to do what the Holy Spirit tells me to do in this course. There aren't too many people who are teaching these things today, and as an older woman, I am to teach younger women to be keepers in their

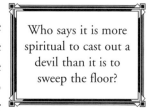

Who says it is more spiritual to cast out a devil than it is to sweep the floor?

---

[14] I heard of a lady who had four children and she was working outside the home. When her husband figured the car expenses, the extra clothing, and the lunches, she was actually bringing home $1 a day. He told her she was worth more than $1 a day at home and wanted her to be the keeper of the home.

home, to be good morally, and to love their husbands and their children.

Father, seal this lesson in the heart of ladies who have read this chapter. I pray that they will look around their home and say, "Holy Spirit, show me what can I do to make this a place of refuge that my family is happy to come home to." Amen.

Nuggets from Chapter 6

As women, we have the privilege and the blessing of being a sweet-smelling fragrance of Christ in our homes as well as in public.

We taught about the virtuous woman having no part of idleness, gossip, discontentment, or self-pity (see Proverbs 31:27).

The virtuous woman has a right attitude in the home toward her husband and toward her children. God wants her to enjoy her roles as wife and mother. Sometimes the woman's attitude is heavier than the work she has to do. A right attitude will lighten the load!

The word "wife" comes from the root word "weaver." Women have the responsibility to weave love, joy, peace, and longsuffering, as opposed to self-pity, into the atmosphere of their homes.

We taught about not letting perversion or negative things come into the home through the television that you wouldn't allow to come in your front door.

As mothers, women should discipline the children after the first time of speaking to them rather than yelling at them numerous times with no results. Good communication with the children will help to create a peaceful atmosphere in the home.

We emphasized the importance of putting your priorities in order by making a list and completing the most important goals first.

We taught on the steps to take to have an orderly home, and the importance of doing four basic things first in the daily routine:

- Making the bed,
- Doing the dishes,
- Wiping the bathrooms, and
- Picking up the clutter.

In this area we talked about involving the children and giving them some responsibilities to complete that are appropriate to their age level.

We talked about women not allowing an attitude of drudgery to have any place when completing repetitive daily household chores.

We taught on the importance of the woman being feminine, not being too independent, and enjoying the husband's masculinity – allowing him to be the lover, leader, protector, and provider that God ordained him to be.

CHAPTER 7

How To Disagree Without Being Disagreeable

Isn't that a good title? I believe the Holy Spirit will help us to learn how to disagree without being disagreeable with one another.

Proverbs 31:31 says, **"Give her of the fruit of her hands, and let her own works praise her in the gates [of the city]!"**

I want to review the scripture from which the title of my course was taken:

> But thanks be to God, Who in Christ always leads us in triumph [as trophies of Christ's victory] and through us spreads and makes evident the fragrance of the knowledge of God everywhere.
> For we are the sweet fragrance of Christ [which exhales] unto God, [discernible alike] among those who are being saved and among those who are perishing.
>
> 2 Corinthians 2:14,15

That is a promise! Christ always leads us in triumph. We are going to win, and everywhere we go we should leave a sweet-smelling fragrance that is discernible alike to all people. When you get squeezed in a situation, the fragrance of the knowledge of God will flow out of you. It will cause you to be a winner in life if you will let that sweet-smelling fragrance flow out of you in every situation in life.

I am teaching in this chapter on how to disagree without being disagreeable. I believe that as you go about as wives and as women, you can prepare a meal and you can set a beautiful table, but if your attitude is stinky or raunchy, it is going to smell bad. It is going to smell like the meat is spoiled, the vegetables are spoiled, and no one is going to enjoy it. Let me encourage you as you go about your family and life's responsibilities to learn to be a person who exhorts, encourages, and praises.

You will notice in the lesson today I talk about filling people's cups with praise. Do not fill them with friction, disapproval, or criticism. Be a person who fills people's lives with good things and not negative things.

I am reading a little book that my daughter-in-law sent to me, just loaned to me, that her little daughter, Stacy, gave her for Mother's Day. It is by Emily Barnes who happens to be one of my favorite writers and it is called, *Fill My Cup, Lord.* I have been very sensitive as I have read it. There were about six or eight cups in the book.

Then I read about not allowing another person to fill your cup with negative things. They may say things, but you just pour that bitter brew right down the sink and fill your cup right back up with God and with what God says about you. It is also important to fill other people's cups with good things. Do not be a part of the bitter cup that they have to drink. You be sure that what you put in the cup is good. So praise is important. It is the lubricant of relationships.

One morning my husband was riding his exercise bicycle instead of walking. I was fixing breakfast at the time. His bicycle began to squeak. I said, "That thing needs some WD-40." He asked if I had some. I always have my WD-40 as it fixes everything. Sometimes it fixes too good. I got the WD-40 and he sprayed it on those little squeaks and it quit squeaking.

Well, praise is the lubricant of relationships. It reduces friction and increases wear. So when your relationship begins squeaking, get out your ten good things you wrote about your husband and put some praise on that relationship.

Clean Up Your Mouth

The first step on how to disagree without being disagreeable is to make sure that corrupt communication does not come out of your mouth.

Ephesians 4:29 says, **"Let no foul or polluting language, nor evil word nor unwholesome or worthless talk [ever] come out of your mouth, but only such [speech] as is good and beneficial to the spiritual progress of others, as is fitting to the need and the occasion, that it may be a blessing and give grace (God's favor) to those who hear it."**

This is your checklist on the kind of talk that comes out of your mouth. I call this my mouthwash scripture. Let this be a gauge for you when family comes at holiday seasons. Let no foul or polluting language come out of your mouth. I thought foul or polluting language was profanity or dirty stories, but it is not.

Listen again to what this verse says: **"Let no foul or polluting language, nor evil word nor unwholesome or worthless talk [ever] come out of your mouth. . . ."** Then it says what to do. **"But only such [speech] as is good and beneficial to the spiritual progress of others. . . ."** That means that everything we say should build someone up spiritually and not tear them down even if they are wrong and deserve to be corrected. We can correct our children in a spiritual and wholesome way without telling them they are dumb, stupid, or a brat.

Let me give you some words to eliminate from your vocabulary:

"You never do it right."
"You never do it unless I tell you to."

"You always make us late."

"You always forget."

"Never," "always," and "ought to" should be eliminated from your vocabulary. I can tell you it will drive them from what you are trying to do. In a child's heart, it will cause rebellion. In a husband's heart, it will bring resentment and cause him to do his own thing. I realize none of us will get 100 percent on this, at least I don't as I forget. That is the reason for lessons like these. We all have to be reminded.

Those are strong words, but corrupt communication is anything that does not minister grace to the hearer.

It is simple! Whatever you say should edify or minister grace. We all need grace in our lives. Do unto others as you would have done unto you. If you are not getting much grace and mercy in your life, I wonder how much grace and mercy you are giving out. Look over those things and do not be so critical or harsh about things others do. Get the corrupt communication out of your vocabulary.

How To Handle Anger Without Sinning

Ephesians 4:26 says, **"When angry, do not sin; do not ever let your wrath (your exasperation, your fury or indignation) last until the sun goes down."**

I believe God gave us the emotion of anger, but I do not think He gave it to us to fight each other. I think He gave it to us to fight the devil and be angry and upset about the evil that is in the world today. I do not think God ever intended us to have anger toward each other. In fact, I believe that when you have anger and it comes out of your mouth and becomes an action, that is when it is sin. Thank God, though, that we can confess our sin and He will forgive us. Do not use that for an excuse to let just everything come out of your mouth.

The next time you get angry, ask yourself this simple question, "Why is this upsetting me?" A lot of times we will find out that our motive for being upset is selfish, because somebody is not doing something the way we think they should. Why am I upset about this? Now, if it is sin, that is different. Then when you let something come out of your mouth, or before it comes out, ask yourself, "Is this kind?" or, "Is this going to edify or minister grace?" "Is this going to help the situation?"

James talks about the tongue.[15] He says it is like a rudder on a ship that can turn the whole thing around and cause it to go in an opposite direction. He talks about it being a spark in the woods that sets the whole forest on fire.

Have you ever said one little thing that started such a fight that you wondered, *Where did this come from?* It was because you took a match and lit the thing and caused the whole thing to flame. How many times have you wanted to take it back, get the fire extinguisher, and put it out, realizing you did not need this kind of fire?

The devil does not like Easter, Thanksgiving, or Christmas. I know the devil wants to get you in strife and division during the holidays. And he doesn't like families. In fact, he is not interested in destroying the church; he is after the family because the family was the first institution founded by God. And if he can destroy the family, he has got the church.

Satan comes against families, so you need to be aware. The Scripture says, "Know your adversary, the devil. Know his plans. Know that he is going to try to get your husband to get up and be grouchy on Thanksgiving morning and ruin the whole day if you let it." But you know what? The best thing to do for that is to take him a cup of coffee, or take him back to bed and close the door so he can rest longer, or do something to get him in a good mood. Do not act the way he does, because the devil will try to get you to become angry.

---

[15] James 3:4-6 KJV - "Behold also the ships, which though they be so great, and are driven of fierce winds, yet are they turned about with a very small helm, whithersoever the governor listeth. Even so the tongue is a little member, and boasteth great things. Behold, how great a matter a little fire kindleth! And the tongue is a fire, a world of iniquity: so is the tongue among our members, that it defileth the whole body, and setteth on fire the course of nature; and it is set on fire of hell."

Your children or family might come in and start talking and gossiping about each other. You step in. Matthew 5:9 KJV says, **"Blessed are the peacemakers: for they shall be called the children of God."**

You do not enter into the gossip. You do not allow the corrupt communication to come out of your mouth so that you do not come into agreement with the accuser. When you come into agreement with someone who is negative about someone else, you are coming into agreement with the devil, the accuser. He is the accuser of the brethren (Revelation 12:10).

There is power in agreement. If you are agreeing that your husband is a loser, that he is not doing anything right, and you are telling someone else who is listening and agreeing with you, hey, it is no wonder he is a loser. Now, I know I am coming on strong about this, but I tell you that in counseling and experience, first in my own life and then in others, I know what I am talking about. I am not giving you just a bunch of words. I know and I thank God that you hear this truth today.

When you say something, ask yourself, "Was it kind?" Hold your tongue until you can get control. My tongue almost needs plastic surgery from the scars. I mean to tell you, I have had to stick that thing back in my mouth, shut my mouth, and get in someplace where I can pray in the Spirit. But shut your mouth!

If a person can control their tongue, they can control their whole body. So I am saying to you, control your tongue, clench your teeth. Put your hand over your mouth!

Holy Spirit, we give You permission to put a guard on our mouth, that when we begin to speak something that is not kind or is corrupt communication, that You just cram it right back down our throat. Put a strong check-valve on us that we cannot let anything come out of our mouth that would not minister grace and healing to the situation in Jesus' name. Amen.

I have often said, "If God can close the mouth of a lion, He can close our mouths." And He closed the mouths of the lions when

Daniel was in the lions' den. So, hold your tongue until you can get control of things. I have often found that if I can keep control of myself that sometimes I don't even have to say anything.

It is also important to get control of your mind because your emotions are based on what you think on. If you think on something and meditate on it, pretty soon it is going to come out of your mouth. Second Corinthians 10:5 says to cast down the imaginations and bring into captivity every thought that is not according to the Word of God. If you can't do anything, just call on the name of Jesus and pray in the Spirit. Or begin to say, "I am a member of the Body of Christ, devil. You do not have any power over me. I am going to overcome this evil with good." *Make that a goal in your life.* That is how we can handle the emotion of anger without sinning.

Ephesians 4:15 says, **"Rather, let our lives lovingly express truth [in all things, speaking truly, dealing truly, living truly]. Enfolded in love, let us grow up in every way and in all things into Him Who is the Head, [even] Christ (the Messiah, the Anointed One)."**

What this verse is saying is, "Speak the truth in love." When you get your emotions calmed down, when you get your tongue in control, if there is something that needs to be dealt with, go back to the situation at the right time (timing is so important) and speak the truth in love.

Say, "Honey, when you did that," or, "When you said that the other night (and take responsibility for your own feelings), it made me feel like I am not doing a good job as your wife." Or, "When you said that about the dinner I cooked, I really tried hard to please you. I really thought that was the way you liked your food cooked. I am sorry. I will try to do better, but it made me feel inadequate as your wife." Make sure the situation is cleared.

> Truth without love is too harsh and cold. Love without truth will not accomplish anything.

This is different than him saying, "You didn't cook my steak the way I like it," and you say, "Well, I hope you choke.

Cook it yourself next time." Even if you want to say that, it is better to say, "I really tried hard to please you."

Or, the husband comes home late for dinner and you have dinner cooked and waiting. Someone caught him in the foyer of the church and the soup is already on the table getting cold. You have put it back in the microwave three times. He comes in the door, sits down, and you want to say, "I hope you enjoy your dinner," but out of the abundance of your heart you say, "I hope you choke on your dinner. I hope it is cold." No! That is not what you do. You are to speak the truth in love.

How can human beings overcome the tendency to be angry? Ephesians 4:23 says, **"And be constantly renewed in the spirit of your mind [having a fresh mental and spiritual attitude]."** You have to constantly renew your mind. It is not a one-time deal. I want to tell you that if I don't constantly think on things that are good, perfect, loving, and of good report; if I don't constantly be aware to keep my mind in the right direction, then I am going to have a negative attitude. I am not going to overcome the emotion and I am going to be angry. My flesh will get strong. We all have opportunities to overcome. So you have to be constantly renewed in the spirit of your mind.

Romans 12:1,2 KJV says:

> **I beseech you therefore, brethren, by the mercies of God, that ye present your bodies a living sacrifice, holy, acceptable unto God, which is your reasonable service.**
> **And be not conformed to this world: but be ye transformed by the renewing of your mind, that ye may prove what is that good, and acceptable, and perfect, will of God.**

I believe the emotion of anger comes from people wanting to control, wanting people to do things their way. I think we as women especially have to deal with a controlling spirit. (I think men sometimes have to deal with controlling spirits too.) I am not putting women down. I believe it happened back in the garden. I think most women have to deal with a controlling spirit.

If people will not do the things as you want them done, then you have the emotion of anger on the inside. You have to be constantly renewed in your mind. You have to recognize that you are trying to control. If it is not sin, what makes it right or wrong? (Example: Whether you put the toilet tissue on this way or whether you put it on that way.) It is not sin. It is just the way you would like to have things done.

There are so many little things you can get upset about and pretty soon that knot gets in your stomach, that knot of emotions. You are upset with people you live with. You are upset with other people. And you really do not know why you are going around upset all the time. It might have started with a very little thing. *You need to present your body a living sacrifice, holy and acceptable unto God, which is your reasonable service and be not conformed to this world, but be transformed by the renewing of your mind.* Keep your mind fresh and renewed spiritually and mentally!

Romans 12:9-12,14,16-18 says:

> [Let your] love be sincere (a real thing); hate what is evil [loathe all ungodliness, turn in horror from wickedness], but hold fast to that which is good.
>
> Love one another with brotherly affection [as members of one family], giving precedence and showing honor to one another.
>
> Never lag in zeal and in earnest endeavor; be aglow and burning with the Spirit, serving the Lord.
>
> Rejoice and exult in hope; be steadfast and patient in suffering and tribulation; be constant in prayer . . .
>
> Bless those who persecute you [who are cruel in their attitude toward you]; bless and do not curse them . . .
>
> Live in harmony with one another; do not be haughty (snobbish, high-minded, exclusive), but readily adjust yourself to [people, things] and give yourselves to humble tasks. Never overestimate yourself or be wise in your own conceits.

> Repay no one evil for evil, but take thought for what is honest and proper and noble [aiming to be above reproach] in the sight of everyone.
>
> If possible, as far as it depends on you, live in peace with everyone.

All things are possible. If you do the possible, what is God going to do? The impossible! So, I believe it is a goal to keep pressing toward the mark of the high calling. We all have a high calling on our lives, and we are pressing toward that mark.

Learn to live in peace one with another. It is easy to live with people who are easy to live with. That is no big deal. It is the people who rub you the wrong way that are hard to get along with. The people you live with a lot of times can just get up and get your day started wrong. But with the Spirit of God on the inside of you, you can overcome.

Ephesians is such a good book of teaching on how to get along with one another and enjoy one another. But after it says, **"Let no foul or polluting language"** (v. 29), there are verses 30 and 32:

> And do not grieve the Holy Spirit of God [do not offend or vex or sadden Him], by Whom you were sealed (marked, branded as God's own, secured) for the day of redemption (of final deliverance through Christ from evil and the consequences of sin) . . .
>
> And become useful and helpful and kind to one another, tenderhearted (compassionate, understanding, lovinghearted), forgiving one another [readily and freely], as God in Christ forgave you.

This is how you can overcome the tendency to be angry.

Satan's Number One Tool to Open Your Home to Every Evil Work

James 3:16 is a key verse for the lesson in this chapter. This is the verse that set me free. We are going to find out what Satan's number one tool is for opening your home to every evil work.

158

I want you to get a fresh vision of keeping the front door closed, sealed with the blood of Jesus, against Satan's number one tool. I encourage you sometime in the next two days to just sit down and study the third chapter of James.

James 3:16 says, **"For wherever there is jealousy (envy) and contention (rivalry and selfish ambition), there will also be confusion (unrest, disharmony, rebellion) and all sorts of evil and vile practices."**

When strife is in your household, the front door is wide open for the devil to come in and steal. This is why Satan tries to get you divided. We often say, "He will steal anything that is not nailed down with the Word of God."

I believe he will steal your material things first. He will cause your cars to break down. He will cause things to happen in your house – accidents and things like that. I can tell you from experience, it happens.

When a lot of situations start coming against us, Bill and I (we don't even know if we have done anything wrong or not) will take hands, pray, and repent, ask God to forgive us and help us get the door closed so the evil one can't steal from us.

The longer the door is open, the more destruction Satan will cause if you do not repent. He will get in with sickness and disease. There are two instances that are imprinted on my memory that I will never forget as long as I live. God used them as teaching tools in my life that when people stayed in strife, they lost their lives. The devil will eventually kill you. That is why strife is so deadly. Strife is not a luxury you can afford. You had better be sure what you are in strife over is worth the price you will pay for it.

In one instance, the child's life was gone, and in the other, the woman who was in strife had her life taken. When picked up off the highway, she was speaking in tongues. She was a Bible school student. I believe she is in heaven today, but she was in strife. She was in a divorce situation, in strife with her husband, and she had set her mind that was the way it was going to be. A drunk driver crossed the center line, hit her head on, and she was killed.

Don't be in strife. I pray that I can paint such a black picture of strife that it will take a lot to push you over and get you in that situation. So, if you are a quick pushover, you be quick to repent. *Do not allow strife to get into your household.*

You can be right or you can be wrong, but if your husband does not make it right, then you make it right. You go to him and say, "Honey, let's close the door. We do not want strife in our household."

Go through your household and run strife out because where there is envy and strife, there is confusion and every evil work. Don't let your children stay in strife. If they start fighting, go to them, get their hands, and say, "Let's pray about this."

My mother used to make us kiss and make up, and at the time we thought it was awful. But I am saying, make them hug and make up. They may hate it, but let them know that is what they are going to have to do if they get into strife, because you are not going to have strife in your house.

What is strife? Strife is a lack of love. How can I say that? Because First Corinthians 13:4-8 is about love and tells you how to act. What are the rules for existence free from strife? This lesson will save your life. It will save your home.

Luke 6:35-38 says:

> But love your enemies and be kind and do good [doing favors so that someone derives benefit from them] and lend, expecting and hoping for nothing in return but considering nothing as lost and despairing of no one; and then your recompense (your reward) will be great (rich, strong, intense, and abundant), and you will be sons of the Most High, for He is kind and charitable and good to the ungrateful and the selfish and wicked.

So be merciful (sympathetic, tender, responsive, and compassionate) even as your Father is [all these].

Judge not [neither pronouncing judgment nor subjecting to censure], and you will not be judged; do not condemn and pronounce guilty, and you will not be condemned and pronounced guilty; acquit and forgive and release (give up resentment, let it drop), and you will be acquitted and forgiven and released.

Give, and [gifts] will be given to you; good measure, pressed down, shaken together, and running over, will they pour into [the pouch formed by] the bosom [of your robe and used as a bag]. For with the measure you deal out [with the measure you use when you confer benefits on others], it will be measured back to you.

This is the way to live a peaceful life. Aren't you glad God left us a handbook to tell us how we can press toward the mark of His high calling?

Ephesians 5:1 says, **"Therefore be imitators of God [copy Him and follow His example], as well-beloved children [imitate their father]."**

Then, verse 2 tells us how to do it: **"And walk in love, [esteeming and delighting in one another] as Christ loved us and gave Himself up for us, a slain offering and sacrifice to God [for you, so that it became] a sweet fragrance."** When you have that forgiveness in your life, when you are willing to block out strife, you become that sweet-smelling fragrance of the love of God in your life.

What is the everyday instruction for walking without strife? Paul writes in Ephesians 4:1-3:

I therefore, the prisoner of the Lord, appeal to and beg you to walk (lead a life) worthy of the [divine] calling to which you have been called [with behavior that is a credit to the summons to God's service,

Living as becomes you] with complete lowliness of mind (humility) and meekness (unselfishness, gentleness, mildness), with patience, bearing with one another and making allowances because you love one another.

Be eager and strive earnestly to guard and keep the harmony and oneness of [and produced by] the Spirit in the binding power of peace.

These are the instructions that we have for living a life free of anger and strife.

I will give you an example about a young man whom we know personally. He went to work for a certain company at a very meager salary doing a small job. He worked in the same room with two other young men. They did not have a kindred spirit, but he did try to have a good relationship with them.

One day when the other two men went to lunch, one of the men left his computer on which showed a letter he had written to the other man about our friend. Our friend read it and found that there had been many negative things that were being said about him. They were stabbing him in the back. He printed the letter and took it home with him. He prayed over the letter, went back, and kept doing his job, believing God to take care of the situation.

In a few weeks' time, that young man was called into the office. The boss told him of a job opening and said, "We have been watching how you get along with people. We want you to have this advancement." He was able to double his salary. He chose not to do anything about two persons and let God handle the situation for him.

God wants you to learn to walk in this manner. If you have hurt feelings or situations in your family, you need to walk in love as First Corinthians 13:4-8 tells you. Let's read it:

Love endures long and is patient and kind; love never is envious nor boils over with jealousy, is not boastful or vainglorious, does not display itself haughtily.

It is not conceited (arrogant and inflated with pride); it is not rude (unmannerly) and does not act unbecomingly. Love (God's love in us) does not insist on its own rights or its own way, for it is not self-seeking; it is not touchy or fretful or resentful; it takes no account of the evil done to it [it pays no attention to a suffered wrong].

It does not rejoice at injustice and unrighteousness, but rejoices when right and truth prevail.

Love bears up under anything and everything that comes, is ever ready to believe the best of every person, its hopes are fadeless under all circumstances, and it endures everything [without weakening].

Love never fails [never fades out or becomes obsolete or comes to an end]. . . .

That is love – God's love. *Agape* love. We cannot have that kind of love on our own. You might say, "I just don't have that kind of love. I just cannot do it."

Do you have the Spirit of God on the inside of you? If you do, Romans 5:5 says He pours His love inside of you. **"God's love has been poured out in our hearts through the Holy Spirit. . . ."** *You need to let the Spirit of God pour His love into you.*

Galatians 5:22 says one of the fruit of the Spirit is "love." So you do have that love inside of you. Love is an unselfish concern that freely accepts another and speaks only of his or her good. How important it is to have that kind of love. Romans 5:8 says that God commended His love toward us while we were yet sinners.

Again, I repeat. *How important the love of God is in our lives!*

Last but not least! I want us to read Matthew 18:21-35:

Then Peter came up to Him and said, Lord, how many times may my brother sin against me and I forgive him and let it go? [As many as] up to seven times?

Jesus answered him, I tell you, not up to seven times, but seventy times seven!

Therefore the kingdom of heaven is like a human king who wished to settle accounts with his attendants.

When he began the accounting, one was brought to him who owed him 10,000 talents [probably about $10,000,000].

And because he could not pay, his master ordered him to be sold, with his wife and his children and everything that he possessed, and payment to be made.

So the attendant fell on his knees, begging him, Have patience with me and I will pay you everything.

And his master's heart was moved with compassion, and he released him and forgave him [cancelling] the debt.

But that same attendant, as he went out, found one of his fellow attendants who owed him a hundred denarii [about twenty dollars]; and he caught him by the throat and said, Pay what you owe!

So his fellow attendant fell down and begged him earnestly, Give me time, and I will pay you all!

But he was unwilling, and he went out and had him put in prison till he should pay the debt.

When his fellow attendants saw what had happened, they were greatly distressed, and they went and told everything that had taken place to their master.

Then his master called him and said to him, You contemptible and wicked attendant! I forgave and cancelled all that [great] debt of yours because you begged me to.

And should you not have had pity and mercy on your fellow attendant, as I had pity and mercy on you?

And in wrath his master turned him over to the torturers (the jailers), till he should pay all that he owed.

So also My heavenly Father will deal with every one of you if you do not freely forgive your brother from your heart his offenses.

Hold out your hands and arms straight and clinch while reading. When finished, release. This is only a short time, but how good it feels when you are released. Back hurts, headaches, tension, and many illnesses are caused by long-term unforgiveness and bitterness.

164

Today, only you know if you have unforgiveness or bitterness in your life. If you have things in your life that need to be released and let go, forgive that person who has hurt you. How important it is that we forgive.

Let forgiveness flow. Forgive that family member, those children, and forgive yourself. God has forgiven us a tremendous debt that we owed. We owed a debt we could not pay. We didn't have enough money to pay this debt. But He paid a debt He did not owe. He took our place. Today, let forgiveness flow through you. It cannot be your natural ability. It has to be the love of God that is poured in your heart that will heal the brokenness.

You have to let God clean your cup of all bitterness. Let that forgiveness flow. Be rooted in love (God's love) and not in bitterness. When you forgive someone, you release them and yourself from the past. When you do not forgive, you keep them bound and you are bound to the circumstance. It is still controlling your life.

You might say, "You just do not understand. You do not live in my house. You have not had the things done to you that I have." I am not saying that I have lived in your house, but Jesus has. He will give you the grace and mercy to forgive, to release, and to let go of every situation that has hurt you. Not only that, but God's love will protect you.

Remember John, how they could not kill him? They tried to. They put him in chains, they boiled him in oil, they did everything to him, but he was protected by the love of God. He was called the apostle of love.

I want to pray for you: *Today, in Jesus' name, I loose that love and protection into your life. I loose that anointing in your life, that supernatural power that will help you do a natural job in a supernatural manner to bring about supernatural results. For this is the day of new beginnings.*

You have stumbled and fallen and you have tried. But today the Spirit of the Lord is telling you to get up. He has given you strength. He has given you mercy today to begin to walk in that love that He so ordained for you.

Today, forgive for all the wrongs, for every negative word that has been spoken, for every time agreement with the accuser has come in.

Forgive us for loss of hope, for we know that our hope is in You, Lord. Our strength is in You, Jesus. Not in the person, not in the situation, but in You, Jesus. You are more than enough. Let each woman feel that love poured into her life today. Warm each woman who is cold. Melt every hard heart, in Jesus' name. Amen.

Nuggets from Chapter 7

In this chapter, we discovered how to disagree with your husband, as well as with others, without being disagreeable. One way is to be an encourager, an exhorter, and a praiser – a person who fills people's lives with good things and not negative things.

Another key we taught is to clean up your mouth and take control of it, using Ephesians 4:29 as your "mouthwash" scripture. Alleviating corrupt communication is anything that does not minister grace to the hearer.

We taught about handling the emotion of anger and speaking the truth in love. We must constantly renew our minds with the Word of God so our thoughts and words line up with God's thoughts and words (Romans 12:1,2 KJV).

The devil's number one door opener into the home is strife. We taught on how to eliminate it from your marriage and family and from every area of your life. We shared incidents of people who were in strife dying prematurely because of it.

Since strife is a lack of love, we taught on living in the God-kind of love as taught in First Corinthians 13:4-8, plus the importance of loving your enemies (Luke 6:35-38), and giving no place to unforgiveness and bitterness in your life.

CHAPTER
8

Picture of the Heavenly Family

(Let's Put it All Together)

Isaiah 61:10 KJV says, **"I will greatly rejoice in the Lord, my soul shall be joyful in my God; for he hath clothed me with the garments of salvation, he hath covered me with the robe of righteousness, as a bridegroom decketh himself with ornaments, and as a bride adorneth herself with her jewels."**

You are the bride of Christ – adorned with the jewels that you have been studying about in the previous chapters.

Isaiah 61:9 KJV says, **"And their seed shall be known among the Gentiles, and their offspring among the people: all that see them shall acknowledge them, that they are the seed which the Lord hath blessed."**

You can have the children who will be known among the nations. They shall be known to be ones who will make up the bride of Christ.

In the previous seven chapters, I taught about your being a capable, intelligent, and virtuous woman. Also, the value of knowing who you are in Christ. This information is very important, and I trust you wrote the twenty good things about yourself, because you cannot be the woman God wants you to be until you know who you are in Him. I gave you Hosea 4:6 regarding people being destroyed for lack of knowledge.

I also taught how to understand and accept the man. It is so important to realize that men are created to have different values, goals, and understanding than women. *There are a lot of things you now understand, because you know the difference in men and women.*

You also learned that men's pressures in life are different than yours and how to accept your husband just as God made him. I trust you wrote the ten good things about him and made the "look" signs to remind you to look to his better side, and also to allow for mistakes. You were also to ask your husband for three things about you which he wanted changed.

I taught regarding your inner and outer beauty, both personal and in your home. Last but not least, I taught on how to disagree without being disagreeable.

This teaching will show you how to be the woman, the wife, and mother you desire to be; to have a happy, peaceful home, not only for your family, but also for visitors in your home.

> I gave you a portrait of the virtuous woman and a goal for which to strive.

Recently, we had a visitor in our home who called from another state after arriving back at her home, stating that she just loved being in our home because she could feel the peace of God there. She also commented on the fact that we did not seem rushed, that we had taken time for our Bible reading and prayer.

Another benefit in learning the teachings of this book is that your prayers will not be hindered. First Peter 3:7 KJV says, **"As being heirs together of the grace of life; that your prayers be not hindered."**

There is so much division, unforgiveness, abuse, mistrust, vying for the rule in the families of the world. Our main goal should be to give people a picture of a Christian family who has love, joy, peace, and forgiveness, along with a close fellowship not only with the heavenly Father, but with each member of the family. In fact, we should be such an example that it would cause them to desire the God-kind of life.

Jesus said in Mark 9:50 KJV, **"Have salt in yourselves, and have peace one with another."** What does salt do? It not only seasons, it preserves, and it can make you thirsty for a drink of water. We should be such an example that unsaved families would thirst to have the kind of life we have.

Jesus said in John 14:2,3 KJV:

> **In my Father's house are many mansions: if it were not so, I would have told you. I go to prepare a place for you.**
> **And if I go and prepare a place for you, I will come again, and receive you unto myself; that where I am, there ye may be also."**

Let us show the world God, the heavenly Father, who is our Father; Jesus, who not only is our Savior but our elder Brother; and the Holy Spirit, who is with us constantly, guiding us, comforting us, and helping us in every area of our lives.

One of these days we will be in our heavenly home, living in everlasting joy with the Father, Jesus, and the Holy Spirit, and all the Christians who have gone before us.

> Our family is to be a picture of the heavenly family. The world needs to see this picture in our lives and homes.

171

Nuggets of Truth

- Hosea 4:6 KJV says, "My people are destroyed for lack of knowledge. . . ."

- Marriages may be made in heaven, but the maintenance is up to the couple.

- God does not love Janet and Bill any more than He loves any person reading this book.

- We don't have to be taught manipulation. We have to be taught that our heart motives should be right and to do our husbands only good as long as there is life within us.

- You cannot love other people properly unless you love yourself and see yourself as being valuable and precious.

- Jesus is saying to you today, "Righteousness is all wrapped up and paid for – the best gift you will ever receive!"

- Holy Spirit, seal the scriptural truths in this lesson in the minds of each reader.

- An investment was made in you, because you are valuable and precious, and God loves you.

- Righteousness is not something you can earn. It comes because of what Jesus did when He died on the cross, took the keys of death and hell, rose from the dead, and ascended on high.

- Accepting a man does not mean to be blind to his mistakes. The answer is to look for the best in him and allow for mistakes.

- I am convinced that men could hear from God a lot easier if wives would get out of their ear.

- Your husband needs reverence, respect, and sex.

- "And ye shall know the truth, and the truth shall make you free" (John 8:32 KJV).

- Just like you as a woman never get too old to be treated like a sweetheart, men never get too old to be admired. They need you to admire what they do.

- Accepting a man does not mean to be blind to his mistakes. The answer is to look for the best in him and allow for mistakes.

- Nothing is really secure except your relationship with Jesus Christ.

- The Holy Spirit will lead you to compliment your husband and build his self-esteem.

- When there is a lack, sometimes it makes your husband feel like a failure as the provider.

- Two wrongs do not make a right.

- Ladies, our position in the home is like the Church is to Christ. What is the

Church doing? Preparing for Christ to come.

- *Remember, a man wants to fulfill his role, and he wants his wife, more than anyone else in the world, to appreciate his achievements and honor him.*

- *You are not to be in competition with your husband. You are to complete him.*

- *A man is responsible to provide the necessities – shelter, food, and a minimal amount of clothing.*

- *Wives, you have a lot more to do with your husbands' success than you realize.*

- The God-given role for the man is: Lover, Leader, Protector, and Provider.

- Never underestimate the power of words. Men really want your approval.

- We should be a sweet-smelling fragrance in every area of our life – spirit, soul, and body.

- An ideal woman will see to it that her household is covered with the Word of God

- Make sure your family is clothed in scarlet – the blood of Jesus.

- The stronger your spirit, the weaker your flesh.

- It doesn't cost a penny to smile, and you will feel better.

- A change in your attitude will change the atmosphere in your home.

- "But as it is written, Eye hath not seen, nor ear heard, neither have entered into the heart of man, the things which God hath prepared for them that love him" (1 Corinthians 2:9 KJV).

- My goal in this chapter is to help you have a different attitude regarding your home.

- Women have the ability to set the atmosphere in their home.

- *Purpose – Goal – Priorities – Planning*

- *God made us women, and women are special!*

- *Who says it is more spiritual to cast out a devil than it is to sweep the floor?*

- *Truth without love is too harsh and cold. Love without truth will not accomplish anything.*

- *Our family is to be a picture of the heavenly family. The world needs to see this picture in our lives and homes.*

A Word From Bill Lay

I will never forget that Sunday morning. While it was over thirty years ago, I can remember it like it was yesterday. That picture of Janet coming home from church with our young boys is still etched in my mind. She came in calmly and began fixing Sunday lunch. No slamming of doors, no banging of pots and pans, just quietly going about the business of preparing our Sunday meal. That was scary! It jerked the slack out of my proud neck. I didn't know how to deal with that kind of an attitude. I hadn't gone to church with her, and I knew that was one of the things she desired for us to do – to go to church as a family.

While I did not know it, this was the first of many changes that was about to occur in our home. Without question, the change in Janet's attitude had a profound impact on changing my life. I began changing from an individual being primarily concerned with making my mark in life to one who was concerned for my family, and ultimately, a ministry.

These principles which Janet first learned, then lived, and later put on paper, today are known as *The Fragrance of Knowledge*. This teaching brought a peace into our home like nothing else did. Ultimately, it brought fulfillment into our lives and was responsible for helping to propel us into the ministry. It changed us from being a family of survival to a family of significance.

Over the years I have seen Janet teach the principles of *The Fragrance of Knowledge* to thousands of women who then enjoyed similar success that we enjoyed in our lives. These principles can be applied in anyone's life.

181

I remember the frustration of not knowing or understanding the difference between a woman's perspective and a man's perspective of what life was all about. Janet and I both desperately wanted to have a good marriage, a good family life, and be "successful." But in our minds, those pictures of how to achieve success were so different.

Without knowing the "how-to's" of achieving these goals, we were continually frustrated. Unfortunately, both of us believed that "our way" was the "right" way. As knowledge came, frustration left, and our lives were changed for the better. We both desperately wanted to have a good, fulfilling marriage. We both desperately wanted to raise our children to be good, healthy, productive children. But what we didn't know was what it took to make it work.

Without this knowledge, we spent a lot of nonproductive years trying to achieve these goals of happiness, joy, fulfillment, and peace, which God intends for each of His children.

Today, I know *The Fragrance of Knowledge* includes God's principles. Janet has a unique gift of being able to express these principles in a way that is easily understood by women. She has demonstrated this over the years with her teaching. Because they are God's principles, they will work for anyone who will apply them.

There is a spiritual law that says, "Whatever you sow, you are going to reap." Most of us do not realize this has application in a marriage as well as in financial matters. Janet did, and because she was willing and obedient, we are enjoying the fruit of the application of these principles in our lives.

In fact, the life I enjoy today with Janet, our family, and the ministry, is a direct result of applying God's principles which she has shared in this book. Without a doubt, Janet is one of the most capable communicators I know, especially with women. I have seen her live, teach, and present the truth which has set thousands of women free.

You see, I am a product of *The Fragrance of Knowledge*.

About the Author

Janet Lay and her husband, Bill, pastored Cornerstone Church in Grove, Oklahoma, for thirteen years. During this time the church enjoyed substantial growth.

Janet and Bill have been married for fifty years. They have four sons, two daughters-in-love, and five grandchildren.

Janet has been active as a teacher, counselor, seminar speaker, and television hostess. For seventeen years she traveled throughout the United States presenting the victorious lifestyle to women. During this time she has spoken in Women's Aglow and Women Alive retreats and meetings. Due to her extensive travel, she has kept abreast of the Holy Spirit's moving among women. She has also ministered in South America, Central America, Canada, and Europe.

Bill joined her in traveling and they conducted marriage seminars for years, touching hundreds of hurting people and seeing lives and marriages restored. They served as Assistant Pastors at Victory Christian Center, Tulsa, Oklahoma, establishing the Counseling Center, with Janet teaching "Marriage and Family" at Victory Bible Institute and serving as Staff Counselor. She is a licensed and ordained minister through Victory Christian Center.

In 1998, Janet was inducted into the Daniel Webster High School Hall of Fame, the school from which she graduated. She received this honor as a result of her counseling and teaching family values. She is noted in the *Who's Who of Oklahoma Counselors.*

Janet has authored and published her self-improvement course for women, *The Fragrance of Knowledge,* based on Proverbs 31. An expanded and amplified version of the book is now available. *The*

Fragrance of Knowledge, First Edition, has been taught in at least seven foreign countries and all over the United States.

Janet's lifelong passion has been to enhance family values. It is her prayer that the truths in this book will enhance your Christian life and enrich your marriage.

Janet has a message for today's women, and she believes ***nothing is impossible with God!***

You may order additional books and tapes
by writing

Faith Family Ministries
3119 Buffalo Lane
Grove, Oklahoma 74344 U.S.A.

You may also receive a free list
of tapes, minibooks, and albums
by writing to the same address.

The six-tape series,
The Fragrance of Knowledge,
from which this book was taken,
is available on cassettes for $30.

New Book Coming Soon!
Hearing the Voice of the Shepherd

NOTES:

NOTES:

NOTES:

NOTES:

NOTES:

NOTES:

NOTES:

4823465BR00115

Made in the USA
San Bernardino, CA
20 April 2017